—

EDITED BY RICHARD W. ETULAIN,
SARA VAUGHN GABBARD, AND
SYLVIA FRANK RODRIGUE

Praise for *Lincoln and the War's End*

"With his effort here, Waugh has created a small gem, one that is easily admired and hard to imitate. Brevity is a virtue, sometimes the most important one for the harried, book-reading public. This latest contribution to the Concise Lincoln Library certainly proves that point, perhaps as well as any in that fine series." —**Matthew Pinkser,** *Journal of Illinois History*

"Waugh excels at writing accessible, entertaining historical prose, and with *Lincoln and the War's End,* the Concise Lincoln Library has a book that will entice casual readers and perhaps inspire them to dig into deeper works."
—**Gerald J. Prokopowicz,** *Journal of Southern History*

"*Lincoln and the War's End* is a must read for all, not just historians."
—**Wallace Dean Draper,** *Journal of the Illinois State Historical Society*

"Waugh's observations about Lincoln's character, motives, decisions, and actions prove to be exceptionally well researched and astute. Supporting quotations from notable figures, both private and public, seem brilliantly selected and uniformly useful. The text, delivered in clear, precise, and well-reasoned prose, is accompanied by ten helpful illustrations, and the whole of the book is attended by excellent notes, an extensive bibliography, and a thoroughly comprehensive index. Students as well as casual readers should find the book to be a fine record of a period which Lincoln's private secretary, William O. Stoddard, called 'that terrible furnace time, during which the old nation melted away, and a new nation was moulded.'"
—**Phillip Parotti,** *Texas Review*

"What John Waugh does as well as almost anyone in the Civil War history business is to build smart narratives around compelling quotations. Like the good reporter he used to be, Waugh collects and evaluates striking reactions from his sources and then weaves them together with deft prose. The result for a short book about the end of the Civil War is pure joy for anybody who wants to immerse themselves in a Lincoln-sided view of that critical period. Give yourself a long plane ride or a quiet weekend at home, and this little volume offers an antidote to some of the anxieties of the modern age. . . . With his effort here, Waugh has created a small gem, one that is easily admired and hard to imitate. Brevity is a virtue, sometimes the most important one for the harried, book-reading public. This latest contribution to the Concise Lincoln Library certainly proves that point, perhaps as well as any in that fine series." –**Matthew Pinsker,** *Journal of Illinois History*

"In a vivid recounting of the critical five months between Lincoln's reelection in November of 1864 and Lee's surrender at Appomattox in April of 1865, John C. Waugh combines a thoughtful analysis of political activities with a vibrant, fast-paced narrative of the military campaigns to illuminate the almost breathtaking denouement of the Civil War."

—**Craig L. Symonds,** author of *Lincoln and his Admirals*

"Bravo to master storyteller John Waugh for this fast-paced and enthralling account of the Civil War's decisive final weeks! A lifetime of research and writing on this endlessly compelling topic is evident in his presentations of the crucial players and decisive battles. His smoothly conversational narrative, and talent for seasoning it with personality studies, eye-catching quotations, and even weather reports, sent me from cover to cover in just one intensely focused sitting."

—**Richard A. Baker,** coauthor of *The American Senate: An Insider's History*

"In the hand of a master historian and storyteller, even a timeless tale can be enlivened and made to sing. The ending is of course unchanged, but with beautiful prose resting on a firm foundation of essential research and his unimpeachable expertise, Waugh educates and entertains."

—**Lynda Crist,** editor of *The Papers of Jefferson Davis,* Rice University

"With a narrative style that is at times moving and dramatic, Waugh expertly weaves together events on the battlefield and in Washington to demonstrate the important connections between military and political history."

—**Carole Emberton,** *Journal of the Abraham Lincoln Association*

"Waugh's work roughly covers the period of Lincoln's reelection until his untimely death, ending on the somber realization that Booth robbed Lincoln of seeing his work completed. Waugh demonstrates the president's confidence in the final days of his life." —**Daniel W. Farrell,** *Civil War History*

"With fitting quotes from many participants during the era, including George Templeton Strong, Mary Boykin Chestnut, and Lincoln's secretaries—John Nicolay and John Hay—the narrative comes alive. [Waugh] uses beautiful prose based on his expertise and research."

—**Frank J. Williams,** *Civil War Book Review*

"In *Lincoln and the War's End,* John C. Waugh writes about Lincoln's role in the final five months of the Civil War. Waugh reminds readers that Lincoln's reelection in 1864 was a 'watershed in American history.' No president had been reelected to a second term since Andrew Jackson in 1832. Most importantly, Lincoln's election came in the midst of a civil war: the Constitution worked." —**Patricia Ann Owens,** *The Annals of Iowa*

JOHN C. WAUGH

Lincoln and the War's End

Southern Illinois University Press
Carbondale

Southern Illinois University Press
www.siupress.com

27 26 25 24 4 3 2 1

First printed 2014.
First paperback edition 2024.

The Concise Lincoln Library has been made possible in part through a generous donation by the Leland E. and LaRita R. Boren Trust.

Cover illustration adapted from a painting by Wendy Allen. *Frontispiece*: Lincoln, 1865—the "sad face" of "one whose heart was sick with hope deferred." Courtesy of the Library of Congress, LC-USZ62–8812.

The Library of Congress has catalogued the 2024 paperback edition and the 2012 hardcover and ebook editions as follows:
ISBN 978-0-8093-3961-7 (paperback)
ISBN 978-0-8093-3351-6 (cloth)
ISBN 978-0-8093-3352-3 (ebook)

Printed on recycled paper 

SIU
Southern Illinois University System

To Abraham Lincoln, for the pleasure of getting to know him in my lifetime

CONTENTS

ILLUSTRATIONS

LINCOLN AND THE WAR'S END

PROLOGUE: WORTH MORE THAN A BATTLE WON

November 8, 1864, was a watershed in American history, marking an epic passage. The Union had voted and, in the midst of a nation-threatening civil war, had reelected Abraham Lincoln as president.

Reelection of a president to a second term was not without precedent, but it had become rare. Not since Andrew Jackson in 1832 had any chief executive been returned to office. Reelection in the midst of a bloody civil war, however, was unique. Never before, at such a time in such circumstances, had such a thing happened anywhere in the world.

A collective surge of gratification swept over those who had voted for Lincoln. Union Party faithful were parading, while Democratic headquarters were darkened. "Thank God it is thus," a Washingtonian penned in his journal, "for it is the salvation of the Country."[1] "*Laus Deo*!" (Praise be to God), a diarist in New York wrote. "The crisis has been passed, and the most momentous popular election ever held since ballots were invented has been decided against treason and disunion."[2] The *New York Herald* said, "The whole North was never more united upon any question than it is at this moment upon the subjugation of the rebellion."[3]

The young Adams brothers of Massachusetts, Charles Francis Jr. in Washington and Henry in London, sons of Charles Francis Adams Sr. and grandsons of John Quincy Adams, exchanged congratulations.

"We do not see that [the election] has left us anything to be desired," Charles Francis Jr. wrote Henry. "[It] has relieved us of the fire in the rear and now we can devote an undivided attention to the remnants of the Confederacy." Henry agreed: "It was one of those cases in which life and death seemed to hang on the issue, and the result is so decisive as to answer all our wishes and hopes."[4]

From Union army headquarters at City Point in Virginia, Ulysses S. Grant, Lincoln's general in chief, wired congratulations to the president, saying, "The election having passed off quietly, no bloodshed or riot throughout the land, is a victory worth more to the country than a battle won." The *Herald*, though often a critic of the president, conceded that "this extraordinary railsplitter enters upon his second term the unquestioned master of the situation in reference to American affairs, at home and abroad."[5]

Lincoln's secretary of state, William Henry Seward, said, "The election has placed our President beyond the pale of human envy or human harm, as he is above the pale of human ambition. Henceforth all men will come to see him as we have seen him—a true, loyal, patient, patriotic, and benevolent man. . . . Abraham Lincoln will take his place with Washington and Franklin and Jefferson and Adams and Jackson—among the benefactors of the country and of the human race."[6]

Late on election night, while the outcome was not yet certain, Lincoln responded from a window in the White House to celebrating serenaders clamoring for a speech. "I cannot at this hour say what has been the result of the election," he told them. But "as now seems probable," the result "will be to the lasting advantage, if not to the very salvation, of the country." He continued, "If I know my heart, my gratitude is free from any taint of personal triumph. I do not impugn the motives of any one opposed to me. It is no pleasure to me to triumph over any one; but I give thanks to the Almighty for this evidence of the people's resolution to stand by free government and the rights of humanity."[7]

Two days later the outcome was certain, and an impromptu procession, "gay with banners and resplendent with lanterns and transparencies," surged around the entrance to the White House for "as far as the eye could reach," the reporter and Lincoln friend Noah Brooks observed. "Bands brayed martial music" and "the roar of cannon shook the sky." Lincoln appeared again at a White House window and a din of welcome greeted him. Tad, the president's irrepressible eleven-year-old son, flew from window to window. Lincoln read from a written speech, believing, as Brooks reported it, "that the importance of the occasion would give it significance, and he was not willing to run the risk of being betrayed by the excitement of the occasion into saying anything which would make him sorry when he saw it in print."[8]

The election, Lincoln told the cheering crowd, "was a necessity. We can not have free government without elections; and if the rebellion could force us to forego, or postpone a national election, it might fairly claim to have already conquered and ruined us." The canvass just decided "has demonstrated that a people's government can sustain a national election, in the midst of a great civil war. Until now it has not been known to the world that this was a possibility." But, Lincoln said, "the rebellion continues; and now that the election is over, may not all, having a common interest, re-unite in a common effort, to save our common country?"[9]

His intent now was to end the war and bring about that reunion of the common country. But this would be more easily said than done.

C H A P T E R   O N E

ARMIES ON THE MARCH

After the election, all eyes turned to two battlefields.

In the East, at Petersburg, Virginia, the Union army commanded by Lieutenant General Ulysses S. Grant had General Robert E. Lee's Confederate Army of Northern Virginia pinned down in a five-month-long siege. The wind on November 13, 1864, was high and raw on the Petersburg line, bringing with it the season's first snow flurries. In his headquarters tent, pitched on a bluff at City Point "without any pretensions to display," Grant was shaping plans for closing out the war.[1]

Lincoln's young assistant personal secretary, John Hay, felt that he knew what the general in chief was thinking. "Grant," he penned in his diary, "is strongly of the belief that the rebel army is making its last grand rally," as Lee had reinforced his own army at Petersburg to some extent and Jubal Early's in the Shenandoah Valley to a lesser extent. Grant "does not think," Hay wrote, that the Confederates "can sensibly increase their armies further. He says that he does not think they can recover from the blow he hopes to give them this winter." Hay also volunteered his own thoughts, his own take, on what the war had come down to as the end appeared to be in view: "I cannot but think that we, having passed through the worst of our trouble and our distress, are now coming out into the faithful promise of assured success. The mists of doubt and danger are under our feet & the rest of the fight we may hope, is to be in the sunshine."[2]

In the West, in the Union army commanded by Major General William Tecumseh Sherman, the mists of doubt and danger were also lifting to the hope of sunshine, darkened only by momentary hesitation about what to do next. After a summer-long campaign beginning at Chattanooga on May 8, Sherman had seized Atlanta on September 2. But he still had the Confederate Army of Tennessee under General John Bell Hood and two pesky Confederate cavalry commanders, Nathan Bedford Forrest and Joe Wheeler, to contend with. They were out there somewhere, still dangerous and doubtless planning mischief, still very likely full of fight.

Sherman could chase after Hood, attempting to corner him and destroy his army. But that idea had little appeal for him. "It will be a physical impossibility," he wrote Grant, "to protect the roads now that Hood, Forrest, and Wheeler, and the whole batch of devils are turned loose without home or habitation."[3] Something else quite out of the ordinary had been growing big in Sherman's mind. He could send heavy reinforcements to Major General George Thomas in Nashville and let him deal with Hood and the rest of the batch of devils. He, with his own sixty thousand hardened veterans, would march the other way, across Georgia to the sea instead, devastating the heart of the rebellion along the way. In his heart of hearts, that was now what Sherman wanted to do.

However, there was a rub: he had to sell the idea to Grant. He set about doing that in early October. "I could cut a swath through to the sea," he argued, "divide the Confederacy in two, and be able to move up in the rear of Lee."[4] He knew he could do it. He told Grant, "I can make the march, and make Georgia howl."[5]

Grant was skeptical. On November 1 he wired Sherman, "Do you not think it advisable, now that Hood has gone so far north, to entirely ruin him before starting on your proposed campaign? . . . If you can see a chance of destroying Hood's army, attend to that first, and make your other move secondary."

Sherman immediately countered. "No single army can catch Hood," he telegraphed Grant the next day. "I regard the pursuit . . . useless." Hood was moving in his own country, so unencumbered that he could make two miles to Sherman's one. In a follow-up wire to Grant that same day, Sherman argued, "I am clearly of the opinion that the best results will follow my contemplated movement through Georgia."

Grant was finally won over. "I say, then, go as you propose," he wired Sherman. For the first time the general in chief had sanctioned and ordered the march to the sea. Now the ball was bouncing cleanly in Sherman's court, and it was not entirely clear to him just when and how to proceed. "I saw the move in my 'mind's eye,'" he later confessed, but "was in doubt as to the time and manner."[6]

The doubt was short-lived. He wired Grant on November 6 that he was ready to march as soon as the election was decided. He set November 10 as the starting day.

Meanwhile, Hood's strategy had also changed. When it became apparent that Sherman was not following him for a fight and perhaps was planning a march in another direction instead, Hood reverted to Plan B. He would not pursue Sherman either but would march instead into Tennessee, hoping to rout Thomas at Nashville, then push "by rapid movements" into Kentucky and continue to the Ohio River to threaten Cincinnati, recruiting troops to strengthen his army as he went.[7] He ordered twenty days' rations for the soldiers in his army and a heavy reserve of artillery to accompany them. By October 31, a month after leaving Sherman's front at Atlanta, he was in Florence, in northwest Alabama on the south bank of the Tennessee River.

On November 9, with Lincoln reelected, Sherman issued special field orders to his sixty-thousand-man infantry and fifty-five-hundred-horse cavalry. The army was to divide into two wings and march on four parallel tracks, living off the country as it went. He ordered his army to "forage liberally," taking what they wanted but leaving each family in the army's path "a reasonable portion for their maintenance." No abusive or threatening language was to be sanctioned. "In districts and neighborhoods where the army is unmolested," he ordered, "no destruction of [private] property should be permitted." However, where they met with hostility or opposition, they were to inflict "a devastation more or less relentless."[8]

Sherman, the man whose brain was said to be "a splendid piece of machinery with all the screws loose" and whose army made the most famous march in military history. Courtesy of the National Archives, photograph no. 111-BA-1674.

It was not until November 16 that Sherman finally launched his army out on the Decatur Road from Atlanta to "make all Georgia howl."[9] The following day he rode out of the city himself, leaving it shattered and burning behind him, a smoldering disaster, with "wrecked engines, bent and twisted iron rails, blackened ruins and lonesome chimneys," and "saddened . . . hearts."[10] Looking back as he rode away, Sherman saw "black smoke rising high in [the] air, and hanging like a pall over the ruined city."[11]

The heavens, one Union officer said, were "one expanse of lurid fire."[12] Another wrote, "The night, for miles around was bright as mid-day; the city was one mass of flame. . . . All the pictures and verbal descriptions of hell I have ever seen never gave me half so vivid an idea of it, as did this flame-wrapped city to-night."[13]

As Sherman's army turned its back on Atlanta and faced toward the sea, a band broke into the rolling strains of "John Brown's Body," which had become the marching song of the army—the Union soldiers' anthem—played to the tune of the old camp meeting melody "Say, Brothers, Will You Meet Us?"[14] The soldiers leaving Atlanta caught up the chorus, and their collective voices soared into a beautiful sunlit fall day as they sang:

> John Brown's body lies a mouldering in the grave,
> John Brown's body lies a mouldering in the grave,
> John Brown's body lies a mouldering in the grave,
> His soul is marching on.
> Glory, Glory, Hallelujah! Glory, Glory, Hallelujah! Glory, Glory Hallelujah!
> His soul is marching on.[15]

Sherman thought he had never heard the chorus sung "with more spirit, or in better harmony of time and place." He detected in his army "an unusual feeling of exhilaration . . . a feeling of something to come, vague and undefined, still full of venture and intense interest"—a devil-may-care feeling. None of them knew exactly the path they were taking, not even Sherman, but he divined the general sentiment of his army to be that they were "marching for Richmond, and that there we should end the war."[16]

As the army marched out of the wrecked city, newly freed black refugees fell in behind, swarming "in immense numbers."[17] "Where are you going, aunty?" one soldier asked a black woman who was carrying a child and making her way through teams of horses, herds of cattle, and marching soldiers. She answered, "I'se gwine whar you'se gwine, massa."[18] There was exhilaration there, too.

Hood at Florence on the Tennessee River no longer cared where Sherman and aunty were going. He had his own direction mapped out. Quixotic strategies were afoot. Two great armies at war generally march toward one another. In this case, however, they were marching away from one another in opposite directions into one another's territory.

Sherman had launched his army into Georgia toward the sea on November 16, but it was taking Hood longer to invade Tennessee. He had been delayed three weeks at Florence awaiting supplies from Corinth, Mississippi. On November 21, five days after Sherman had left for the sea, Hood finally set his thirty-six-thousand-man army marching across the river into Tennessee.

Hood's immediate target was Union major general John M. Schofield's twenty-two-thousand-man infantry force waiting at Pulaski, twenty miles across the Tennessee line in the direction of Franklin and Nashville. His hope was to get in the rear of Schofield by rapid marching toward Columbia on the south bank of the Duck River above Pulaski, cut him off, and destroy him before he could reach Nashville. Schofield, who had been Hood's classmate at West Point, was under orders from General Thomas to slow Hood's march into Tennessee as long as possible without risking a general engagement. Thomas's intention was for Schofield to cross the Harpeth River at Franklin, hold Hood in check there, and retire gradually into Nashville, where Thomas was gathering reinforcements and digging in.

As Hood's army moved toward him, Schofield evacuated Pulaski and headed for Columbia, twenty-eight miles to the north, some twenty miles from Franklin and sixty miles from Nashville. It became a parallel race of the two armies for the Duck River crossing. Schofield reached it first and held there until the night of November 29. Somehow, however, he had to get to Franklin as ordered, and it would have to be through Hood's army, now gathering around him.

In a daring move on the moonless night of November 29, Schofield pushed his entire force silently through Spring Hill, fifteen miles above Columbia on the Franklin road. His army crept silently past Hood's unsuspecting Confederates, whose campfires burned within eight hundred yards of the road, within earshot, within gunshot range—"straight past a thousand gleaming fires," a Union soldier wrote, under a "star of 'good luck'" that "twinkled upon Schofield's army out of the midnight sky."[19]

Riding with his army, falling asleep in the saddle, Schofield arrived at Franklin before dawn on November 30. There, on a bend on the south bank of the Harpeth, he dug in on a two-mile-long crescent, with both flanks resting on the river. It had been a close shave getting through at Spring Hill. Figuratively mopping his brow, Schofield wired Thomas in Nashville, "The slightest mistake on my part, or failure of a subordinate, during the last three days might have proved disastrous. I don't want to get into so tight a place again."[20]

Hood awoke that morning to learn of the shocking midnight passage of the enemy through his army. He was chagrined and mortified. He called letting Schofield slip through in the night a "fearful blunder," saying bitterly, "We had held [them] within the palm of our hands."[21] The chance to cut off his enemy's every avenue of escape had slipped away, a close call that a Union officer believed "may well be set down in the calendar of lost opportunities."[22] Humiliated, driven by a passion to recoup, rout his enemy, and drive Schofield into the Harpeth, Hood sent his army marching rapidly toward Franklin in the early morning hours of November 30.

A Hood lieutenant, Brigadier General Benjamin F. Cheatham, reconnoitered the Federal position "in the lap of the Harpeth."[23] "I do not like the looks of this fight," he told Hood; "the enemy has an excellent position and is well fortified." He recommended against a frontal attack.[24]

The sad-eyed Hood was only thirty-three years old, though he looked older. Shell fragments taken at Gettysburg had damaged the nerves and muscles of his left arm and rendered it useless. A musket ball at Chickamauga had cost him his right leg, amputated at the hip. He had to ride strapped to his saddle. But he was a fighter, and he had come to fight. Despite his generals' advice not to make a frontal charge against such formidable entrenchments, he intended to attack.

Now, on an Indian summer afternoon "misty with the mellow light of autumn," his army halted on the southern edge of the town.[25] By midafternoon the entire Confederate line was stretched in battle array, colors fluttering and muskets gleaming. At four o'clock on November 30, on the verge of the twilight of an early sunset, the Confederate mass "began to quiver from right to left, and to move like an advancing storm cloud over the open plain."[26] Its bugles blaring and its drums pounding, it swept on toward the Union line, "as steady and resistless as a tidal wave," as one Union officer described it.[27] Another officer said it looked like a "human battering ram . . . a huge monster closed in folds of flashing steel."[28] Backed against the Harpeth, Schofield stared at the attacking line and found the sight breathtaking—"the grandest display possible in war," a "scene of indescribable grandeur." Despite its grandeur, however, it was a thoroughly ill-advised, ill-conceived assault. Only two of Hood's three corps were present, they had virtually no artillery support, and the force was ill positioned. When it struck, the scene of grandeur quickly changed to what Schofield described as "one of most tragic interest and anxiety."[29]

The Confederates, a Union colonel recalled, advanced in a wild rush driven by a "rebel yell" rising high above a "Yankee cheer" and "threw themselves against the works." There was not a breath of wind, he said, and dense smoke settled on the field. Through "this blinding medium," Hood launched assault after assault.[30]

A hundred wagonloads of ammunition, artillery, and musket cartridges hurled at the Confederate line had produced the smoke, plunging the field into "sudden darkness," a Union officer wrote, "like an eclipse."[31] Along part of the battle line, "a blaze of fire leaped from the breastworks and played so incessantly that it appeared to those who saw it as if it had formed a solid plane upon which a man might walk." A Confederate staff officer described it as "a continuous living fringe of flame."[32] "It seemed to me the air was so full of bullets that I could have caught some by simply grabbing on either side or above me," a Union officer said. "Five times the rebel columns charged that little army in the bend of the Harpeth. Five times they went back shattered and broken."[33]

The fighting across the Union works became "fiendish," a "private soldier's battle."[34] It was "almost hand to hand for two mortal hours," one soldier wrote.[35] In the fiery assaults one after another, six Confederate generals were killed, six wounded, and one captured. "The death-angel," a Confederate soldier said, "was there to gather its last harvest."[36] Edward Porter Alexander, a Confederate artillery officer, later wrote, "There is no assault in military history, of which I have ever heard, that equals this in the loss of generals engaged upon the side of the assailants."[37]

The slaughter did not end until about ten o'clock, "in the darkness of the night," leaving in the silence only the wail of the wounded lying "in the agonies of death" between the lines, "so near that the outstretched hand could almost reach them."[38] A Confederate staff officer summed it all up: "In the reckless disregard of life, and in tenacity of purpose displayed, the attack has rarely been equaled, never exceeded."[39]

As the battle ended and the crack of the last gun died away, Schofield moved quickly to execute the final part of his orders. He had his army moving out of its entrenchments across the Harpeth by midnight—again in the dark of night—marching to join and reinforce Thomas. By morning on December 1, he was settled in the shelter of the works at Nashville, on Thomas's left flank.

The charge at Franklin had been reckless, and Hood had paid a monumental price. Not only had he lost key generals and other field officers in the futile attack, but he was left with only twenty-three thousand of the effective force of thirty-six thousand he had brought to the fight. Perhaps worse, his "cherished plan"[40] to crush Schofield's army before it reached Nashville had utterly failed. And perhaps most devastating of all, as a Union officer suggested, "the vigor, the courage and life of Hood's army was destroyed at Franklin."[41]

Now all that was left for Hood, his flags "tattered, and torn, and battle-riddled," was to follow Schofield to Nashville.[42] This he did, arriving outside the city the next day. There he and his men took up positions some two miles from the city nearly parallel to the Union line, threw up works of their own, invested the town, and waited. Hood badly needed reinforcements, which he expected from Texas in the Trans-Mississippi West. Perhaps with that support, he might yet attack Thomas, whip him, and follow him into his works. Then Hood could get on with his master strategy for Tennessee and Kentucky. It was perhaps a dying hope, but it still lived in Hood's breast.

CHAPTER TWO

UNFINISHED BUSINESS

While George Thomas and John Bell Hood were busy in Tennessee, Lincoln in Washington, which the president's personal secretary, John Nicolay, disgustedly called a "labor-ridden and care-burdened town, whose very atmosphere seems infected with some subtle poison fatal to all peace of mind or repose of body,"[1] was casting anxious looks toward Georgia. "We have talked of elections until there is nothing more to say about them," Lincoln told a serenading crowd on December 6. "The most interesting news we now have is from Sherman." All Lincoln knew about Sherman was that he appeared to be marching through insurgent territory, with the result not yet known.[2]

Sherman was out of telegraphic contact. Nobody in the North knew exactly where he was or where he was going. Lincoln told Sherman's brother John, a senator from Ohio, "I know what hole he went in at, but I can't tell what hole he will come out of."[3] At a White House levee an intimate Lincoln acquaintance reached him in the line. The president greeted him absent-mindedly, with only a conventional passing hand pump. Seeing that he was not recognized, the friend spoke to him again instead of moving on. Suddenly realizing who stood before him, Lincoln seized his hand once more, shook it vigorously, and said, "How do you do? How do you do? Excuse me for not noticing you at first; the fact is, I was thinking of that man down South."[4]

Even Grant, also thinking of "that man down South," had only a vague idea of where he was or where he was going to come out.

"Sherman's army," he confessed, "is now somewhat in the condition of a ground-mole when he disappears under a lawn. You can here and there trace his track, but you are not quite certain where he will come out till you see his head."[5] All that was known in the North for certain was that Sherman was penetrating somewhere into the "bowels of the enemy's country."[6]

Georgians, however, entertained no similar uncertainty as to where the "ground-mole" was. Sherman was devastatingly above-ground in plain sight, blazing a hot trail across the midsection of their state. At first Southerners exulted, seeing in it an opportunity to visit on Sherman's army the fate the Russians had visited on Napoleon's snow-blasted army half a century earlier—its destruction. Before Sherman set out, Confederate president Jefferson Davis had said in a speech in Macon, "Sherman cannot keep up his long line of communication, and retreat sooner or later, he must, and when that day comes, the fate that befel [sic] the army of the French Empire and its retreat from Moscow will be reacted. Our cavalry and our people will harass and destroy his army as did the Cossacks that of Napoleon, and the Yankee General, like him will escape with only a body guard."[7]

When Grant heard of Davis's forewarning of doom for Sherman, the general, a man not ordinarily given to light sarcasm, said, "Mr. Davis has not made it quite plain who is to furnish the snow for this Moscow retreat."[8] Snow or no snow, the Richmond Examiner predicted that Sherman's ill-advised march would only "lead him to the Paradise of Fools."[9]

Those confident Confederate notions were now being disabused, however. Eliza Frances Andrews, a young Georgia woman passing over Sherman's track in what she called "that terrible journey across the burnt country," saw the situation as it was. She wrote of one "poor little village but ruins, charred and black as Yankee hearts."[10]

Sherman's two-pronged army of "black hearts" was marching virtually unchecked across open country roads on its parallel tracks, in "fine and bracing" weather. The army was subsisting as planned off the country, destroying public property, breaking up railroads, twisting ties, and cutting Confederate communications.[11] Its foragers were fanning out daily from the marching columns, plundering the rich Georgia plantations. "Everything on foot and wing, all the things of the earth and air," one of them wrote, "were 'contraband of war.'"[12]

Sherman's march had become what one Union officer called "a grand military promenade," laying "open the heart of the Confederacy."[13] After Sherman had marched past, apparently headed for the Atlantic, one Georgian no longer doubted that his army was an unstoppable juggernaut. "If you had been here and seen the sort of men composing his cohorts," he said, "you would not question that they could go wherever they had a mind to."[14] The Confederates were now calling Sherman "this modern Attila."[15]

On November 23 Sherman's right wing reached Milledgeville, the capital of Georgia, ending the first stage of the march. Georgia's governor and legislature had "hurriedly escaped from one end of the city," a Union officer said, "as we marched in at the other."[16] They "ignominiously fled," Sherman complained.[17] On December 3 his army was in Millen, a hundred miles from Milledgeville and less than eighty to Savannah, which now appeared to be his destination. The road ahead looked clear and wide open.

On December 5 the Thirty-Eighth Congress returned to Washington for its second and final session, to a Capitol building "greatly beautified and purified," canopied anew by an iron-paneled dome rising two hundred feet from the floor.[18] Under it the lawmakers filed in, found their seats, and awaited the annual message from the president.

The message had been pressing heavily on Lincoln's mind, cohabiting strongly with Sherman's whereabouts—more heavily, Secretary of the Navy Gideon Welles believed, "than I have witnessed on any former occasion."[19] Lincoln had started work on the message in mid-November, writing on stiff slips of pasteboard or boxboard—his favorite habit, according to the reporter Noah Brooks, when he wrote "anything requiring thought." With a number of these stiff slips of board at hand, "seated at ease in his arm chair," Brooks explained, "he lays the slip on his knee and writes and re-writes in pencil what is afterward copied in his own hand, with new changes and interlineations. Then being 'set up' by the printer with big 'slugs' in place of 'leads,' spaces of half an inch are left between each line in the proof, when more corrections and interlineations are made, and from this patchwork the document is finally set up and printed."[20]

Before finishing the message, Lincoln urgently needed something from the governors of all the Union states—a tally of "exactly, or approximately" the aggregate of votes cast in each of their states in the late presidential election. Nine of the twenty-four governors still had not complied by the end of November. "May I renew my request?" he pressed them. "My object fails if I do not receive it before Congress meets." Lincoln wanted the figures to show how strong the purpose of the people in the loyal states was to "maintain the integrity of the Union," to show the inexhaustible strength of the North in resources—"in living men"—and the will to persevere to victory.[21]

Armed with the data at last, Lincoln finished his address and sent it to the waiting Congress at one o'clock in the afternoon on December 6. (A president did not deliver his State of the Union address in person in those days; a secretary dropped copies off at both Houses, where a clerk read the address.) In this address, the fourth of his presidency, Lincoln covered a broad galaxy of issues: the state of the Union's foreign affairs, the government's financial standing, the progress of the war both on land and at sea, the condition of the postal service, the well-being of the territories, the distribution of public lands under the new Homestead Law, the progress of rail and telegraph expansion, Indian affairs, aid to solders and their widows and orphans—and his coveted report, with the help of the governors, on the meaning of the election.

"The war continues," Lincoln told the legislators. "Since the last annual message all the important lines and positions then occupied by our forces have been maintained, and our arms have steadily advanced." He pointed to "Sherman's attempted march of three hundred miles directly through the insurgent region" as "the most remarkable feature in the military operations of the year." Still in progress and hard to pinpoint, the march, he said, tended to "show a great increase of our relative strength that our General-in-Chief should feel able to confront and hold in check every active force of the enemy, and yet to detach a well-appointed large army to move on such an expedition." Because its result was still unknown, he declined any conjecture about it.

More clearly known were "important movements" during the year for "moulding society for the durability of the Union" at war's end. The process, Lincoln said, was already under way. Loyal state governments had been organized in insurgent Arkansas and Louisiana. Movements in the same direction, "more extensive, though less definite," were afoot in Missouri, Kentucky, and Tennessee. Maryland was already a "complete success . . . secure to Liberty and Union for all the future."

Then turning to the election data sent him by the governors, Lincoln said, "Judging by the recent canvass and its result, the purpose of the people, within the loyal States, to maintain the integrity of the Union, was never more firm, nor more nearly unanimous, than now. The extraordinary calmness and good order with which the millions of voters met and mingled at the polls, give strong assurance of this."

He told Congress that the election exhibited "another fact not less valuable . . . that we do not approach exhaustion in the most important branch of natural resources—that of living men." Though it is "melancholy to reflect that the war has filled so many graves, and carried mourning to so many hearts, it is some relief to know that, compared with the surviving, the fallen have been so few." The important fact remains, he said, that "we have more men now than we had when the war began; that we are not exhausted, nor in the process of exhaustion; that we are gaining strength, and may, if need be, maintain the contest indefinitely. The natural resources, then, are unexhausted, and, as we believe, inexhaustible. The public purpose to re-establish and maintain the national authority is unchanged, and as we believe, unchangeable."

Lincoln ended the message by citing clearly what would end the war instantly. The president of the insurgent states, he said, would "accept nothing short of severance of the Union—precisely, what we will not and cannot give." It is therefore an issue that "can only be tried by war and decided by victory."

However, Lincoln believed, what is true "of him who heads the insurgent cause, is not necessarily true of those who follow." Some of them, he said, already desire peace and reunion. "They can, at any moment, have peace simply by laying down their arms and submitting to the national authority under the Constitution." In short, "in stating a single condition of peace, I mean simply to say that the war will cease on the part of the government, whenever it shall have ceased on the part of those who began it."[22]

The address was matter-of-fact and it went down well. A sure signal of that was the reaction of Thaddeus Stevens, the Radical Republican congressman from Pennsylvania, one of Lincoln's most unrelenting critics in his own party. Stevens conceded that the message was "the best . . . which has been sent to Congress in the past sixty years."[23]

Lincoln also was having to deal with a cabinet in flux. Four of his original seven members had left or were leaving. Before the election and under pressure from the Radicals, Lincoln had let Postmaster General Montgomery Blair, a conservative they detested, go. Blair had resigned to accommodate Lincoln and make the move easier. The president had replaced him with former Ohio governor William Dennison Jr.

The seventy-one-year-old attorney general, Edward Bates, wanted to retire. He told Lincoln that he wished to step down right after the election. As the last day of November approached, Bates was feeling "a sensible relief, as the lifting of a burden."[24] Lincoln wanted to fill the vacancy with Judge Advocate General Joseph Holt, a Kentuckian who had been the secretary of war in James Buchanan's cabinet.

Holt declined, suggesting that instead he appoint James Speed, a fellow Kentuckian and an old friend of Lincoln's. Acccepting the suggestion, Lincoln wired Speed on December 1, "I appoint you to be Attorney General. Please come on at once"—not giving him much time or choice. Speed wired back, "Will leave tomorrow for Washington."[25] With Speed on his way, Lincoln described him as "one of those well-poised men, not too common here, who are not spoiled by a big office."[26]

Treasury Secretary William Pitt Fessenden, who had succeeded Salmon P. Chase when he resigned in early 1864, was also intending to step down, likely to be succeeded by the able comptroller of the currency, Hugh McCulloch. A fourth departure from the cabinet in the new year would be Secretary of the Interior John P. Usher, likely to be replaced by Iowa senator James Harlan, whose daughter Mary was engaged to marry Lincoln's son Robert. All of these new appointees or expected appointees were personally attached to Lincoln, and none of them aspired to the presidency—unlike Chase, who had been aspiring to it for years.[27]

The changes in the cabinet were transpiring smoothly compared with filling the even more important newly vacated office of chief justice of the Supreme Court. Longtime Chief Justice Roger Taney had died on October 12. Among those said to covet the appointment was the newly resigned Edward Bates and the recently replaced Montgomery Blair. But most heads had turned immediately to Chase, now unemployed, as the obvious front-runner for the job.

A former governor and U.S. senator from Ohio, and Lincoln's able secretary of the treasury for the first three years of the war, Chase had been a less than faithful subordinate. Indeed, he had mounted an aborted undercover campaign early in 1864 to run for president against Lincoln, believing himself far better qualified to run the country than his boss. His campaign, however, crashed in full public view in February. Later, in June, Chase offered his resignation, something he was wont to do on occasion, and Lincoln this time surprised him by accepting it.

Now, with the top job on the court open and Chase without a job, his friends—notably his best friend, the Radical senator Charles Sumner of Massachusetts—began lobbying Lincoln without stint for his appointment. Chase was a particular favorite of the Radicals. They believed not only that he, a Radical himself, was the best suited for the office, but also that the great issues of the war as they saw them would be safest in his hands.[28] Sumner wrote to Lincoln urging Chase's appointment, telling the president there was "a feverishness in the public mind with regard to the Chief Justiceship"—the fever being for Chase, a man whose "interpretation of the Constitution & of the War Powers, would deal a death-blow to Slavery."[29]

Lincoln's friends, however, were more than dubious. Considering Chase personally hostile to the president, they vigorously opposed the appointment. Lincoln said, "My friends all over the country are trying to put up the bars between me and Governor Chase. I have a vast number of messages and letters from men who think they are my friends, imploring and warning me not to appoint him."[30]

Lincoln was not without his own reservations, not necessarily connected with Chase's questionable loyalty. The president told Senator Henry Wilson of Massachusetts, "Of Mr. Chase's ability and of his soundness on the general issues of the war there is, of course, no question. I have only one doubt about his appointment. He is a man of unbounded ambition and has been working all his life to become president. That he can never be, and I fear that if I make him chief justice, he will simply become more restless and uneasy and neglect the place in his strife and intrigue to make himself president. If I were sure that he would go on the bench and give up his aspirations and do nothing but make himself a great judge, I would not hesitate a moment."[31]

None of the tugging and hauling and speculation made any difference. There was not really much of a moment of hesitation in Lincoln's mind. "Now, I know more about Governor Chase's hostility to me than any of these men can tell me," he said; "but I am going to appoint him."[32] Indeed, he said, "there has never been a moment since the breath left old Taney's body that I did not conceive it to be the best thing to do to appoint Mr. Chase to that high office."[33]

So on December 6 he did so, overriding all "remembrance of personal differences and personal wrongs."[34] The Senate unanimously confirmed the nomination at once, the same day, without referring it to committee. Lincoln told his friend Ward Hill Lamon, "His appointment will satisfy the Radicals and after that they will not dare kick up against any appointment I may make."[35]

Lincoln believed it was the right thing to do. Whether he was entirely happy about it was another question. Welles wrote in his diary that Lincoln later confessed to William E. Chandler of New Hampshire that he "would rather have swallowed his buckhorn chair than to have nominated Chase."[36] John Nicolay, Lincoln's young personal secretary, had this take on the appointment: "Probably no other man than Lincoln would have had, in this age of the world, the degree of magnanimity to thus forgive and exalt a rival who had so deeply and so unjustifiably intrigued against him. It is however only another most marked illustration of the greatness of the President, in this age of little men."[37]

So appoint Chase Lincoln did. And with the shuffling of high-level offices done, he turned his attention again to "that man down South." He now knew what hole Sherman had come out of.

CHAPTER THREE

ADVANCE AND RETREAT

On December 10 Lincoln awoke to a Washington buried overnight under a heavy snowfall. Far to the South, Sherman's army that morning was staring at the defenses of Savannah—from a quagmire. "This whole country" around Savannah, one soldier testified, "is a marsh," everything "a black muck"; "nothing," another observer said, but "one vast swamp."[1]

Sherman had driven his exuberant, forager-fed army across more than a third of Georgia—255 miles of the state from Atlanta to the sea, averaging 10 miles a day for twenty-seven days and encountering little resistance the entire distance. And here he was at last before the city he coveted—in a bog perhaps, but by no means bogged down.

"I regard Savannah as already *gained*," he wrote Secretary of War Edwin M. Stanton.[2] And as the snow had invested Washington, he invested the city now at his mercy. His sixty thousand soldiers had its twenty-five thousand citizens and the only organized rebel army in his path—a ten-thousand-man force under the command of Confederate general William Joseph Hardee—penned within.

Sherman had another matter to settle, however, before Savannah could be his: he had to open a new line of supply. That meant making contact with the Union fleet standing offshore. Blocking his way to that end was a fort called McAllister, a huge earthwork armed with twenty-three cannons and a mortar. It was one of the oldest war bastions on the American continent and considered immune to capture. But its guns were mainly bent to the river and sea and not toward the land, and its heralded immunity meant nothing to Sherman's soldiers. They assailed it at five o'clock in the afternoon on December 13, and twenty minutes later it was theirs.

Things had not been moving so fast, however, for George Thomas in Nashville. For two weeks Hood had been digging in before the city, awaiting a Union attack that had not yet come. Also waiting for it, far more impatiently, were the Lincoln administration in Washington and U. S. Grant at City Point. Grant was sending multiple messages to Thomas that escalated in impatience, urging, prodding, directing, then flat-out ordering him to attack.

On December 8, Grant wired Major General Henry Halleck, the army chief of staff in Washington, "If Thomas has not struck yet he ought to be ordered to hand over his command to Schofield." This was a little bit farther than Lincoln wanted to go, however. Halleck wired back that those in Washington, impatient as they felt for immediate action, held Thomas in higher regard than Grant did. "If you wish General Thomas relieved," Halleck told him, "give the order. No one here will, I think, interfere. The responsibility, however, will be yours, as no one here, so far as I am informed, wishes General Thomas removed."[3]

Thomas, a Virginian who had remained faithful to the Union, was an able general, particularly talented at defending a position. His stubborn stand at Chickamauga in September 1863, when the rest of the Union army was retreating to Chattanooga defeated and in disorder, had won him widespread acclaim and a nickname—the "Rock of Chickamauga." But he was also a rock in many other ways, a methodical man, slow to move until ready, known by his West Point classmates as "Old Slow Trot." His fellow officers in the Old Army used to say, "Thomas is too slow to move, but too brave to run away." One of Grant's staff officers said of Thomas, "He was like an elephant crossing a bridge, and feeling his way with ponderous feet before every step." But, it was generally conceded, when he was finally across the bridge, "woe to the enemy he met on the opposite side."[4]

Hunkered in at Nashville, Thomas did not think his army was yet ready to deliver a crushing blow and was feeling his way, elephant-like, until he was satisfied that it was. He was trotting so slowly that Grant, at the end of his patience, penned an order on December 9 relieving him outright and promoting Schofield to command. It was an order not sent, however, for by then a freezing ice storm had locked up Nashville. The ground—fields and roads—were hard frozen under "a continuous glare of ice."[5] Both armies were "ice-bound on the storm-beaten hills."[6]

Ice or no ice, the ever-impatient Grant had then ordered Major General John Logan to Nashville to take command if Thomas did not attack. Not trusting to this alone, Grant left City Point and headed for Nashville himself.

A thaw, meanwhile, had mercifully set in on the night of December 13, and the next night Thomas wired Washington, "The ice having melted away to-day, the enemy will be attacked to-morrow morning."[7]

He meant it. By nine o'clock on the fifteenth a dense fog blanketing the field lifted to reveal a warm, sunny winter morning. The sight of Hood's army lying in wait in unknown numbers was, in the words of a colonel on Thomas's staff, "inspiring."[8] At noon, at long last, uninspired by the sight, Thomas launched an army-killing attack. The elephant in Thomas had crossed the bridge.

More than fifty thousand of Thomas's richly reinforced army of some eighty-two thousand troops struck both flanks of Hood's army. The blow on the right was but a strong feint. The main assault fell like a murderous sledgehammer on the Confederate left. That night Thomas wired Washington, "Attacked the enemy's left this morning; drove it from the river below city nearly to Franklin pike—distance about eight miles."[9] It was a laconic, understated message of electrifying effect.

The next day Thomas sent his entire line forward, crowding Hood's army unmercifully. A rout followed. The sheer weight of Union "men and metal" was too heavy for Hood.[10] His army, "worse clawed" than on the fifteenth, was crushed, "broken and scattered."[11] "Hood's whole army was routed and in full retreat," a Confederate soldier wrote. "Such a scene I never saw. The army was panic-stricken. The woods everywhere were full of running soldiers." Two Confederate generals threw up a line to try to stem the hemorrhage, but the line quickly dissolved. The soldier described it as "like trying to stop the current of Duck river with a fish net."[12]

"Didn't I tell you we could lick 'em?" Thomas exulted to James Harrison Wilson, his cavalry commander. "Didn't I tell you we could lick 'em, if they would only let us alone?"[13]

Word of the stunning Union victory and Confederate rout reached John Logan in Louisville, a day away from Nashville. He stopped; his presence was no longer necessary. Word of it reached Grant, who had reached Washington en route to Nashville. He also stopped, his presence also unnecessary. "I guess," Grant said, "we will not go to Nashville." Instead he wired Thomas, "I was just on my way to Nashville, but [hearing of] your splendid success of to-day, I shall go no farther."[14]

Hood's shattered, routed, and retreating army reached the Tennessee River over hard-frozen roads on a cold, cheerless Christmas morning five weeks after launching its movement to Nashville. Lincoln, who had fretted over the delay too, was delighted with the news. But he wanted more—a devastating pursuit. "You made a magnificent beginning," he wired Thomas. "A grand consummation is within your easy reach. Do not let it slip."[15]

Hood pushed headlong on to Tupelo, Mississippi, and Thomas halted his pursuit at the Tennessee River. He had done more than enough. Hood's hopes of pushing through Nashville to the Ohio River and beyond were crushed with his army. Lincoln was finally able to say, "I reckon that **that** army, **as an army**, won't be of much account hereafter."[16] Indeed, no fighting Confederate army now existed between the Mississippi and the Potomac.

A popular song with Confederate soldiers, particularly Texans, was "The Yellow Rose of Texas," a love song about a heroine of the battle for Texas independence in 1836. Its last verse went like this:

> Oh now I'm going to find her, for my heart is full of woe,
> And we'll sing the songs together, that we sung so long ago,
> We'll play the banjo gaily, and we'll sing the songs of yore,
> And the Yellow Rose of Texas shall be mine forevermore.

After Hood's disastrous rout at Nashville, the last verse was rewritten to fit the situation:

And now I'm going southward, for my heart is full of woe,
I'm going back to Georgia, to find my Uncle Joe,
You may talk about your Beauregard, and sing of Bobby Lee,
But the gallant Hood of Texas played hell in Tennessee.[17]

When Sherman's troops meanwhile had stormed and taken Fort McAllister, this had opened the Ogeechee River to the sea and linked his army to the federal fleet. By December 16 Sherman held Savannah and all of its avenues of supply in a stranglehold. On December 18 an applauding Grant wired Sherman, "I assured [Lincoln] with the army you had, and you in command of it, there was no danger but you would *strike* bottom on salt-water some place."[18]

Two days later the Confederates in Savannah had also struck bottom. That night and through the early morning hours of the twenty-first, General Hardee evacuated the city with his ten thousand men, forty-seven guns, and wagon train. He crossed the Savannah River by a pontoon bridge, blowing up the navy yard as he left and retreating to Charleston. Finding the city evacuated, Sherman's soldiers marched in that day. Sherman rode in the next day and sent a brief message to Lincoln: "I beg to present you, as a Christmas gift, the city of Savannah, with 150 heavy guns and plenty of ammunition, and also about 25,000 bales of cotton."[19]

Lincoln received this blessed gift on Christmas Day, and on December 26 he wired Sherman his thanks:

> When you were about leaving Atlanta for the Atlantic coast, I was *anxious,* if not fearful; but feeling that you were the better judge, and remembering that "nothing risked, nothing gained" I did not interfere. Now, the undertaking being a success, the honor is all yours; for I believe none of us went farther than to acquiesce. And, taking the work of Gen. Thomas into the count, as it should be taken, it is indeed a great success. Not only does it afford the obvious and immediate military advantages; but, in showing to the world that your army could be divided, putting the stronger part to an important new service, and yet leaving enough to vanquish the old opposing force of the whole—Hood's army—it brings those who sat in darkness, to see a great light.[20]

Lincoln, always looking for still more light, added, "But what next?" Then he conceded, "I suppose it will be safer if I leave Gen. Grant and yourself to decide." Sherman was already working on what he would do next. "I am ready for the Great Next," he assured Lincoln, "as soon as I can complete certain preliminaries, and learn of Genl Grant his and your preference of immediate 'objectives.'"[21]

To Grant he wired, "The occupation of Savannah . . . completes the first part of our game."[22] The first part had been spectacular, "resplendent," crowed the *New York Times*.[23] In Savannah, Sherman's army was enjoying "a Christmas Jubilee."[24] Applause was flooding in. The New York lawyer George Templeton Strong wrote in his diary that it was Sherman's "grand adagio movement through Georgia," which "seems to have been among the best and boldest conceptions of the war and to have been most triumphantly executed."[25] A foreign observer called the campaign "a work of genius, marveling that Sherman "surely possesses the sacred fire."[26] The composer and songwriter Henry Clay Work soon immortalized that "sacred fire" with a song:

> Bring the good old bugle boys! we'll sing another song,
> Sing it with a spirit that will start the world along—
> Sing it as we used to sing it, fifty thousand strong,
> While we were marching through Georgia.
> Hurrah! hurrah! we bring the jubilee!
> Hurrah! hurrah! the flag that makes you free!
> So we sang the chorus from Atlanta to the sea,
> While we were marching through Georgia.[27]

For white Southerners, however, it was anything but a jubilee. Instead of the "Paradise of Fools" they had predicted for Sherman, it had been a monumental disaster for them. More Confederates than ever now saw Sherman as "the Attila of the nineteenth century."[28] One South Carolinian, Mary Boykin Chesnut, wrote in her diary of "the deep waters closing over us." While Northerners were calling the fall of Savannah "a magnificent prize," she was calling it "a second Vicksburg business" and writing a dolorous verse:

Darkest of all Decembers
Ever my life has known,
Sitting here by the embers
Stunned—helpless—alone—[29]

On yet another front, the Union deeply coveted the city of Wilmington, North Carolina. When the war came, the South had twelve major ports open on the thirty-five-hundred-mile shoreline from the Atlantic to the Gulf. Wilmington, thirty miles inland from where the Cape Fear River, the largest and most important in North Carolina, emptied into the Atlantic, was now the sole major Southern port still open to Confederate blockade runners. It was the South's only remaining open gateway to the world, except for Galveston in far-away Trans-Mississippi Texas. Wilmington had to be closed. But guarding it were three forts at the river's mouth, chief among them Fort Fisher, the largest seacoast fortification in the Confederacy. The campaign to reduce Fort Fisher, capture the city, and close the port, was launched in late December with a powerful joint naval and land assault.

Situated at the tip of a long-fingered peninsula, Fort Fisher was designed to withstand the heaviest artillery fire and defy capture. It was massive and L-shaped, its seaward face nearly a mile long. Atop its log framework, sand and dirt were piled on twenty-five feet thick and ten to thirty feet high. Forty-seven big guns stared outward from its battlements.[30] Abetting its invulnerability was a deadly line of subterranean torpedoes (mines) buried in the sandy soil some five hundred to six hundred feet from the fort's land face. A mighty Union armada of sixty ships, five of them ironclads, commanded by Rear Admiral David Dixon Porter and carrying six hundred guns, had arrived in sight of Fort Fisher on December 20.

But bombardment awaited a ploy that the Union hoped would dismount the guns on the fort, explode its magazines, destroy its garrison, and make its capture easy. The instrument for this blow was to be a defunct gunboat, the *Louisiana*, loaded with 215 pounds of powder, pulled close in to the walls of the fort, and detonated.

This idea was the brainchild of Major General Benjamin F. Butler, a political general from Massachusetts who was in command of the land forces. Late in the night on December 23 the powder-laden *Louisiana* was run up to within five hundred feet of the fort, and the fuses were lit at one thirty the next morning. But instead of devastating the nearby fort as hoped, the detonation was a monumental fizzle. The fleet lying by in the Atlantic scarcely felt the shock, and the Confederates in the fort believed that a blockade runner loaded with ammunition had exploded or a boiler in the federal fleet had burst. Its effect, as an earlier engineering report had predicted, was about the same as "firing feathers from muskets"—"a mere puff of smoke," complained Secretary of the Navy Gideon Welles.[31]

Smarting from this failure, Porter's fleet opened a massive bombardment of the fort's northeast face on Saturday, December 24. Confederate colonel William Lamb, commanding at Fort Fisher, remembered it as one of those perfect winter days that occasionally dawn on Cape Fear. "The gale which had backed around from the northeast to the southwest," he wrote, "had subsided the day before, and was followed by a dead calm. The air was balmy for winter, and the sun shone with almost Indian summer warmth, and the deep blue sea was calm as a lake, and broke lazily on the bar and beach."

Into this calm came hellfire. "With the rising sun out of old ocean," Lamb wrote, "there came upon the horizon, one after another, the vessels of the fleet, the grand frigates leading the van, followed by the ironclads—more than fifty men of war, heading for the Confederate stronghold." The armada's leading men of war, the *Minnesota*, *Colorado*, and *Wabash*, Lamb called "floating fortresses, each mounting more guns than all the batteries on the land."[32] The sides of the frigates, another observer wrote, "seemed a sheet of flame, and the roar of their guns like a mighty thunderbolt."[33]

The next morning, as news of Sherman's Christmas gift was reaching Lincoln, the great fleet moved in again and Butler landed his army. With his skirmish line advanced to within fifty yards of the fort, Butler saw a still-defiant work, virtually unmoved by the naval bombardment and looking as if it could not be taken by assault. So at the height of the bombardment, he called the whole thing off and began withdrawing his army.

General Grant was furious, calling the campaign "a gross and culpable failure" and a "fearful mistake," saying it had been "abandoned by the army just when the fort was nearly in our possession."[34] Porter and Butler launched a bitter round of recriminations, blaming each other for the failure. A Washington observer called it "the Butler & Porter snarl," describing it as a "hot fight between two gas bags—who may puncture each other."[35]

Not only did this attempt to take Fort Fisher end embarrassingly, but Butler, whose bag was worse punctured, also saw his military career ended. On January 4, 1865, Grant requested that Butler be relieved, and on January 7 Lincoln so ordered it. "BUTLER is dethroned," the *New York Times* wrote on January 11 with more than a touch of satisfaction.[36] Butler was widely considered one of the more maladroit political generals in the war. The *New York Herald* had earlier called him "a first class lawyer" but "only a second rate general."[37] Grant believed him incompetent.

Of Wilmington, the ultimate target of the aborted campaign, Welles wrote in his diary, "We shall undoubtedly get the place, but I hardly know when."[38] Getting it sooner rather than later was in the works. As Lincoln stood greeting a mob of visitors in line at the annual New Year's Day levee at the White House in snow-clad Washington beside a frozen Potomac, he had already ordered a second attempt. From City Point Grant had fired a message to Porter: "Hold on a few days, and I will endeavor to be back with an increased force, and *without the former commander.*"[39]

On the night of January 12 the mighty Union armada, which Lamb believed "the most formidable fleet that ever floated on the sea," returned and opened another hellish fire.[40] This time the armada carried some eighty-five hundred troops, commanded now by Major General Alfred H. Terry, a professional soldier of proven competence. At sunrise the next day, the fleet under Admiral Porter again "rained shot and shell, upon fort and beach and wooded hills, causing the very earth and sea to tremble."[41] It was an "infernal storm," said one army officer.[42]

Over the next two days the garrison's strength was ratcheted up from eight hundred to fifteen hundred men. The Union armada, as Lamb put it, "continued its ceaseless torment" all day and night on

January 13 and 14, bowling "their eleven and fifteen inch shells along the parapet, scattering shrapnel in the darkness," killing or wounding at least two hundred Confederate defenders.[43] Terry, who learned the nature of his assignment only after unsealing his orders aboard ship on the way to Fort Fisher, had meanwhile landed his troops through tumbling surf and approached the fort on the land side.

It looked hopeless to the Confederates under the overall command in the region of General Braxton Bragg. And Bragg had left the fort to survive or fall on its own. Major General William H. C. Whiting, in command of the Confederate Military District of Wilmington, arrived at the fort in the midst of the bombardment and said, "Lamb, my boy, I have come to share your fate. You and your garrison are to be sacrificed."[44]

January 15 dawned, "as lovely a day," a Union naval officer observed, "as ever brightened the earth; [with] a placid sea, whose waves danced and shone like liquid silver."[45] With the rising sun, Terry's command was massed for an assault. The ships of the fleet abruptly stopped their thundering and blasted a charge with their steam whistles, "a soul-stirring signal both to besiegers and besieged," mourned Lamb. Then the attacking columns came, he testified, "like avalanches on our right and left"—Terry's troops from the land side and sixteen hundred sailors and four hundred marines on the fort's sea face.[46]

The sailor-marine assault was repulsed, and the fighting on the land side finally came down to a hand-to-hand, bayonet-bloodied melee that ended in the fort's surrender around ten o'clock that night. Porter's fleet entered the harbor. The editor of the *New York Times* exulted that "the last breathing-hole of the rebellion" had been effectively closed.[47]

For the Confederacy, it was a disaster. Lee had earlier warned Colonel Lamb, "If Fort Fisher falls, I shall have to evacuate Richmond."[48] Alexander Stephens, vice president of the Confederacy, believed that "the fall [of Fort Fisher] was one of the greatest disasters which had befallen our Cause from the beginning of the war—not excepting the loss of Vicksburg or Atlanta." It was, he said, "the complete shutting out of the Confederate States from all intercourse by sea with Foreign Countries"[49]—total suffocation.

CHAPTER FOUR

CONFEDERACY ON THE ROPES

The noose had tightened everywhere. "The widespread treason of the times," the *Washington Star* wrote, "is now happily gasping in death throes."[1] Sherman had made Georgia howl and seized Savannah. Thomas had destroyed the Confederate army in the West. Major General Philip H. Sheridan had devastated the Shenandoah Valley. Grant had Lee penned up in Petersburg. And the final safe harbor for blockade runners had been slammed shut at Wilmington.

The rebellion, wrote one of Grant's lieutenants, "reeled and staggered, like a wounded gladiator."[2] Northern generals, the *New York Herald* said, were "pressing the rebellion to its last shifts."[3] During these winter weeks, one of the Adams brothers, Charles Francis Jr., later wrote in his autobiography, "the flags were incessantly displayed in honor of some new victory."[4] A Confederate bureaucrat in Richmond admitted in his diary, "Disasters have come thick and fast."[5]

The editor of the *New York Times*, Henry J. Raymond, wrote that by year's end, "the whole country had come to regard the strength of the rebellion as substantially broken. . . . The rebels were known to be rapidly and fatally failing."[6] One of Sherman's officers said, "I should think the Johnnys would have enough of this before long."[7]

The awful truth was dawning all over the South. Mary Chesnut, in Columbia, South Carolina, put it this way in her diary: "All the world open to them. We shut up in a Bastille. We are at sea. Our boat has sprung a leak." Mary was looking south toward Savannah with fear and trembling for what she believed was surely coming.

"I sit here," she wrote, "and listen for Sherman's bugles." He will, she cried into her diary, "soon effect a juncture with Grant and leave us a howling wilderness."[8]

Her anguish was well founded. Sherman was looking northward and thinking now of making the Carolinas howl. Within days of entering Savannah, he was telling Grant that it was "as clear as daylight" what he must do next. In a letter to General Halleck, he wrote, "The truth is, the whole army is burning with an insatiable desire to wreak vengeance upon South Carolina. I almost tremble at her fate, but feel that she deserves all that seems in store for her." On December 27 Grant wrote to Sherman, "Without waiting further directions, then, you may make your preparations to start on your northern expedition without delay. Break up the railroads in South and North Carolina, and join the armies operating against Richmond as soon as you can."[9]

On January 2 Sherman authorized the march. The plans were these: Again the army with its sixty thousand men, sixty-eight guns, and twenty-five hundred loaded wagons was to divide as before into two parallel wings. Each of its wagons would be pulled by six mules, its six hundred accompanying ambulances by two horses. The wagons would carry ammunition enough for "a great battle," forage for about seven days, and provisions for twenty days. Cattle would be driven on the hoof; other cattle, hogs, and poultry would be gathered as before by foragers on the line of march. The end destination was Goldsboro, North Carolina, some four hundred miles to the north. Sherman estimated that the march would take six weeks.[10] It was not expected to be easy. In making the Carolinas howl, they could expect stiffer, reinforced Confederate opposition.

Sherman had hoped to start by mid-January, but heavy rains pouring down had pushed the Savannah River over its banks, inundating the roads. Mary Chesnut would not hear the bugles just yet.

In Washington, gratified by the tightening noose, Lincoln had a favor to ask of Grant. His son Robert, now age twenty-two, had been urging his parents to let him go to the war as other young men had been doing. That idea, with its high potential for losing yet another son, petrified Mary Lincoln. She had already lost two: Eddie, who had died in Illinois in 1850 at age three, and Willie, who had died in the White House in 1862 at age eleven. She was desperately opposed to Robert entering the service, with the risk of losing him too. Lincoln, with pressure from these two directions, asked his favor of Grant.

Answer, he told his general on January 19, "as though I was not President, but only a friend." Could Robert, Lincoln asked, "without embarrassment to you, or detriment to the service, go into your Military family with some nominal rank, I, and not the public, furnishing his necessary means?" Lincoln explained that he would like Robert "to see something of the war before it ends," short of being put into the ranks or given a commission "to which those who have already served long, are better entitled, and better qualified to hold."

The general was pleased to accommodate his president. He replied, "I will be most happy to have him in my Military family in the manner you propose." He would make Robert a captain and assistant adjutant general of volunteers as of February 11.[11]

On the same day that Lincoln asked this of Grant, Sherman officially ordered the march into the Carolinas, waiting now only for a weather-willing time to start. Mary Chesnut would soon be hearing the bugles.

CHAPTER FIVE

DEATHBLOW TO SLAVERY

As the new year gained momentum, it was not Sherman's plans or the quickening good fortune on the battlefields of the war that drew Lincoln's immediate attention. It was the four million black people in the country still locked in slavery.

In his heart of hearts, he wanted the lock broken and all slaves set forever free. But it was not that easy, and past efforts had always required careful navigation and compromise, yet they were not met with success. "It is no secret," Lincoln said, "that I have wished, and still do wish, mankind everywhere to be free."[1] He had made a stunning beginning in the summer of 1862 when he drafted a preliminary Emancipation Proclamation, which in its final form took effect on the first day of 1863. But that landmark executive order, as important as it was—and considered by Lincoln as first and foremost a military necessity—had "freed" only the slaves in the Deep South still held in slavery. They would be truly free only as his armies advanced into slave territory or as the slaves succeeded in running away into Union lines.

Besides, the Emancipation Proclamation was a presidential edict, an executive order only. It lacked staying power—the status of legal concrete. After the war was over, it could be ruled illegal in the courts or reversed by a succeeding president. Freedom needed to be expanded to the entire country, North and South, and permanently anchored if it were to be the lasting law of the land. Without that, the end of slavery at war's end was uncertain at best. And it could be argued that if slavery continued, the war may not really be over.

Lincoln now desperately wanted the "peculiar institution," as the South called it, ended with the war. Before he became president he had said, "No man has the right to keep his fellow man in bondage, be he black or white, and the time will come, and must come, when there will not be a single slave within the borders of this country."[2] Lincoln now believed that time had come, and he knew how it must be done: a constitutional amendment—a thirteenth—was needed to set that freedom forever in cement.

An earlier Thirteenth Amendment resolution to do just the opposite had been passed in the heat of the secession crisis in 1861. It would have protected slavery forever, making it perpetual. But with the coming of the war, the states failed to ratify the amendment.

Adding an amendment of any kind to the Constitution since it was framed in 1787 and became law in 1789 was something few had been willing to undertake—even to consider—for the past half century. There had been twelve amendments, but the first ten of those, collectively known as the Bill of Rights, were considered a necessary adjunct, either to clarify the original Constitution or to reassure doubters. They were passed soon after the mother document and ratified in December 1791. The Eleventh Amendment, making states immune to out-of-state and foreign lawsuits, was ratified in February 1795. The twelfth, revising presidential election procedures, was ratified in June 1804. All twelve were viewed as supplementary—resolving something unforeseen rather than changing the original.

Since then, there had been no tinkering with the sacred document and virtually no inclination to do so. It was not easily tinkered with. A constitutional amendment required a two-thirds vote of both houses of Congress and ratification by three-fourths of the states—both Everest-sized summits to climb. But Lincoln in the new year saw the path to a new amendment as an Everest that must be climbed, and climbed now.

There were signs that it could happen. Lincoln's reading of the public pulse told him that. Since late 1863 petitions had been flooding in from around the country. By early 1864 some two thousand men, women, and children Union-wide were chasing signatures to end slavery once and for all. By mid-July petitions bearing nearly four hundred thousand names had inundated Congress, mainly spearheaded by the Women's Loyal National League. No other petition drive for a single objective had ever gathered so many signatures. The first of these petitions did not call specifically for a constitutional amendment, but by early 1864 they were being specific.

As the petitions rolled in, the amendment was introduced in Congress in early 1864 and debate opened in the Senate. Senate Republicans had united behind it. Democrats, with a few notable exceptions, continued to oppose it, fearing that an amendment freeing all slaves everywhere threatened the racial and social order of the country.

As Democratic senator Lazarus W. Powell of Kentucky put it, "I believe this Government was made by white men and for white men; and if it is ever preserved it must be preserved by white men." He also said, "The white man is [the black man's] superior, and will be so whether you call him a slave or an equal. It has ever been so, and I can see no reason why the history of all the past should be reversed."[3] He and most Democrats did not want any of that to change. They saw the proposed thirteenth as an "unconstitutional constitutional amendment"[4] because it would overthrow an institution sanctified by the framers.

Republican rhetoric echoed the argument mounted by Lincoln six years before in his celebrated debates with Stephen A. Douglas in their contest for the Senate seat in Illinois. Senator Timothy Otis Howe of Wisconsin restated it: "Admit that as a race [blacks] are inferior to the race of whites," but "I ask Senators, I ask men if that is a fact which authorizes you or me to enslave them?"[5]

The amendment resolution, ramrodded by Lyman Trumbull, the senator from Lincoln's Illinois, passed the Senate on April 8, 1864, by a vote of thirty-eight to six—eight votes more than the necessary two-thirds. The story was different, however, in the House, which opened debate on the amendment the last day of May. Two weeks later, in a final vote, it failed to win the necessary two-thirds majority.

Throughout the first round of debate in Congress and the resolution's defeat in the House, Lincoln had not interfered. He had not yet been renominated or reelected. He said nothing in support of the amendment publicly. But he was clearly for it. Isaac Arnold, a close friend and congressman from Illinois, said the president was "chagrined and disappointed"[6] when it failed.

However, Lincoln had by no means given up on it. As the Republican nominating convention approached, he threw his weight behind the amendment. Before the convention opened on June 7 in Baltimore, he suggested to New York senator Edwin D. Morgan, the party chairman, who would deliver the opening address, that he make the amendment its cornerstone. He said to Morgan, "We are like whalers who have been long on a chase—we have at last got the harpoon into the monster, but we must now look how we steer, or, with one 'flop' of his *tail*, he will yet send us all into eternity!"[7] Not wanting to be flopped into eternity, Morgan did as Lincoln suggested, and the convention fell in line. The resolutions committee drafted a platform plank to abolish slavery immediately by a constitutional amendment.

The choice in the canvass that followed was clear-cut: The Democratic platform supported the right of the states to authorize and maintain slavery if they wished. The Republican platform called for slavery's "utter and complete extirpation from the soil of the Republic" by way of a constitutional amendment.[8]

Lincoln and his party now clearly saw such an amendment as the answer, the most likely way to solve the problem of making emancipation constitutional forever—if it could be passed. Once his reelection had been secured, and with public sentiment tending in its favor, Lincoln believed that now it could and must be done. As the new year of 1865 dawned, he launched a powerful lobbying campaign for congressional reconsideration and passage of the resolution that had failed in the House the summer before. In his annual message to Congress in early December 1864, he had urged it to take up the amendment resolution again before it adjourned in March 1865. The election had given Lincoln enough votes in the new House that would be convening in December 1865 to get it passed then, but he wanted it done sooner—by the sitting Congress before its adjournment and his second inaugural on March 4. Failing that, Lincoln could call the new Congress into special session to get it done.

But he said to the old Congress, still sitting, "May we not agree that the sooner the better?"[9] Lincoln and Secretary of State William Seward began twisting congressional arms to make it sooner.

The amendment was reintroduced in the House by James M. Ashley of Ohio, its sponsor and leading champion, on January 6, "a pouring rainy day" in Washington.[10] Bitter debate erupted, and for twenty-five days it was touch and go as to whether it would pass. Every Republican member of the House was certain to vote for the resolution. The key was to persuade enough Democrats who had voted against it before to break with the majority of their party and vote for it this time. It called for a touch of logrolling—making certain promises to wavering Democratic members in return for their votes—an art form Lincoln had perfected in his days in the Illinois legislature.

The effort succeeded. Thirteen Democrats broke with their ranks, joining the Republicans and the four Democrats who had voted for it when it had earlier failed. It was a close call right down to the end. The resolution passed in the House the last day of January 1865—by a spare two votes, 119 to 56—to what Lincoln's reporter friend Noah Brooks described as "an explosion, a storm of cheers, the like of which probably no Congress of the United States ever heard before. Strong men embraced each other with tears. The galleries and aisles bristling with standing, cheering crowds. The air was stirred with a cloud of

Scene on the House floor with the passage of the Thirteenth Amendment abolishing slavery nationwide forever; Lincoln called it "a King's cure for all the evils." From the Lincoln Financial Foundation.

women's handkerchiefs waving and floating; hands were shaking . . . cheer after cheer, and burst after burst followed." One of its champions hailed its passage as "the sublime and immortal event."[11]

"It seemed to me," exulted the Republican congressman from Indiana, George W. Julian, a fierce opponent of slavery, that "I had been born into a new life, and that the world was overflowing with beauty and joy." He wrote that he was "inexpressibly thankful for the privilege of recording [his] name on so glorious a page of the nation's history, and in testimony of an event so long only dreamed of as possible in the distant future."[12]

Julian's late father-in-law, Joshua Giddings, the former congressman of Ohio who had died in May 1864, would have been even more "inexpressibly thankful." A ferocious abolitionist, Giddings had worked with Congressman Abraham Lincoln in 1849 on a bill that would have ended the slave trade in the District of Columbia. Lacking key support, the bill was never introduced.

What the resolution now passed said was short and to the point. Its forty-three concise words were lifted wholesale from the Northwest Ordinance of 1787, which had outlawed slavery in the western territories—Illinois, Ohio, Indiana, Wisconsin, and part of Minnesota. The amendment said, "Neither slavery nor involuntary servitude, except as a punishment for crime whereof the party shall have been duly convicted, shall exist within the United States, or any place subject to their jurisdiction," and "Congress shall have power to enforce this article by appropriate legislation."[13]

Lincoln saw the amendment as the looked-for final finisher of the military emancipation embodied in the Emancipation Proclamation in 1863. He called it "this great moral victory" and said it was "a King's cure for all the evils. It winds the whole thing up"—"the consummation of the great game we are playing." It "will clinch the whole subject" and "bring the war, I have no doubt, rapidly to a close."[14] Although it was not legally necessary, the exuberant Lincoln signed the resolution, and it went out immediately seeking ratification by the required three-fourths of the states—twenty-seven of the thirty-six.

The *New York Times* viewed the adoption of the amendment as "the most important step ever taken by Congress." The newspaper believed its ratification would "complete the most important act of internal administration performed by any nation for a hundred years. It perfects the great work of the founders of our republic."[15] It was widely seen as the triumphant end of the antislavery movement—the great reform that would purify the republic, constitutionalize the Declaration of Independence, and extend it to all, irrespective of color.[16] As one of its supporters said, it was a hoped-for "disposing of the Negro question in a constitutional way."[17] It was generally believed that slavery, that "one shrill discord" in the body politic, had been silenced forever—that the "final blow at the crime of slavery has been struck."[18]

When he heard the bells ringing to hail the amendment's passage, the relentlessly abolitionist poet John Greenleaf Whittier wrote:

> It is done!
> Clang of bell and roar of gun
> Send the tidings up and down.
> How the belfries rock and reel,
> How the great guns, peal on peal,
> Fling the joy from town to town![19]

CHAPTER SIX

NEGOTIATING PEACE

As the fate of the Thirteenth Amendment resolution teetered on the edge of either failure or passage in the House, a rumor that could have sent it tumbling into oblivion invaded Washington. The rumor held that Confederate commissioners were at that moment on their way to Washington to negotiate a peace settlement.

This made Ohio congressman James Ashley exceedingly anxious. He was busy striving to engineer the resolution through on the House floor and did not relish this abrupt turn of events. He urgently asked Lincoln if the rumor was true. It was generally believed that if it was, it would surely kill the amendment, sending the urgently courted Democrats "off in a tangent at the last moment had they smelt Peace." Lincoln calmed Ashley. "So far as I know," he told him, "there are no peace commissioners in the city, or likely to be in it."[1] Thus Lincoln saved the amendment—with a reassurance that was true only as far as it went. Confederate peace commissioners were indeed on their way north, but to Fortress Monroe, not Washington—a very fine distinction.

This new turn in the state of affairs was Francis Preston Blair's doing. Blair at age seventy-three was the patriarch of an irrepressibly political family in Washington. He was a venerable figure in the country, a leading political fixture in the capital since the days of Andrew Jackson. He had two sons who were also fixtures. One, Montgomery, had been Lincoln's postmaster general until recently. The other, Frank Jr., was a former Missouri congressman and an able major general commanding a corps in Sherman's army.

The elder Blair thought he knew how to strike a blow for peace. He would go to Richmond and meet personally with Jefferson Davis, an old acquaintance, and talk things out. In December, with that in mind, he requested approval from Lincoln and a pass to go there. Lincoln greatly respected the old man and was not opposed to this gambit. But Blair was in no way authorized to speak for the administration. It would be a strictly private undertaking. Blair wanted to go immediately, but Lincoln told him, "Come to me when Savannah falls."[2]

When Savannah fell, Blair went as suggested to petition Lincoln again, and on December 28, 1864, the president issued Blair a pass to go South and return. Two days later Blair sent a letter to Davis requesting an interview "to explain the views I entertain in reference to the state of the affairs of our country & to submit to your consideration ideas which in my opinion you may turn to good & possibly bring to practical results that may not only repair all the ruin the war has brought upon the Nation but contribute to . . . the welfare of other nations that have suffered from it." He would be coming "merely as a private citizen," he told Davis. "I come to you wholly unaccredited [but with] permission to pass our lines & to offer to you my own suggestions—suggestions which I have submitted to no one in authority on this side." With the hope that it might "lead to something practicable," he said, "I will confidentially unbosom my heart frankly & without reserve."[3]

Davis, who had long known and respected the old man from before the war, agreed to a meeting, and Blair left at once, on January 7, 1865. He checked into the Spotswood Hotel in Richmond, a five-story brick hostelry fronted by an ornate iron façade, where every high-level visitor to the Confederacy stayed. Something of a nerve center of the capital, the place to see and be seen, it was "as thoroughly identified with the Rebellion as the inn at Bethlehem with the gospel."[4] Its basement housed the Confederate post office.

Blair's arrival was a mystery. Speculation abounded over why he had come. The official explanation was that he was there to search for papers taken from his house in Silver Spring, Maryland, during Confederate lieutenant general Jubal Early's aborted raid on Washington in July 1864.

On January 12 Blair met privately with Davis and introduced his proposal: slavery was to be abandoned and Northern amnesty broadened to include all who had engaged in the War of the Rebellion. In a mutually declared armistice, the armies of the two enemies would unite in a joint operation against the French, a common enemy who had taken over Mexico—a nagging worry for both North and South. Blair believed that the plan would have the practical value of uniting the two sections in one common purpose, pulling the warring states together in the name of the Monroe Doctrine.[5]

Davis did not embrace this idea, but talk of bringing the bloodshed to an end had escalated in Richmond by early 1865. Under this mounting pressure for peace, Davis handed Blair a note for Lincoln indicating that he was willing "to dispense with forms and to send or receive commissioners . . . 'to enter into conference, with a view to secure peace to the two countries.'"[6]

Blair hurried back to Washington with this message, which Lincoln received with a good deal of skepticism. But he was willing to give negotiations a try. What he did not care for was Davis's notion that there were two countries. He wrote Blair, authorizing him to tell Davis, "I have constantly been, am now, and shall continue, ready to receive any agent whom he, or any other influential person now resisting the national authority, may informally send to me, with the view of securing peace to the people of our one common country."[7]

Blair left Washington again with this message for Davis on January 20 and presented it the next day. He then returned to Washington, his two visits still stirring curiosity and speculation about what it all meant.

In Richmond, Davis appointed three commissioners—Alexander H. Stephens, vice president of the Confederacy; R. M. T. Hunter, president pro tem of the Confederate Senate; and John A. Campbell, assistant Confederate secretary of war and former justice of the U.S. Supreme Court—and sent them off to cross the siege line in Petersburg and head, they thought, for Washington. They crossed to hopeful cheers from both sides of the line on January 29.

In Washington, Lincoln had cleared passage for them to cross, ordering Grant to let them through "without necessary delay"—not to Washington, however, but to Fortress Monroe, to be met there "in due time by some person or persons" for an informal conference. At the same time, on January 30 Lincoln advised Grant, "Let none of this, have any effect upon your movements or plans." He reiterated that qualifier to Grant on February 1.

He then sent Secretary of State William Seward to Fortress Monroe to meet with the commissioners. Lincoln told Seward to make known to them that three things were indispensable: national authority must be restored throughout all the states, the U.S. president would not retreat on the slavery question, and there would be no cessation of hostilities short of an end of the war and the disbanding of all forces hostile to the government. In short, he was asking for reunion of the Union and the end of slavery—unconditional submission.

Meanwhile, with the Thirteenth Amendment now safely bundled and on its way to the states to be ratified, Lincoln decided, at Grant's urging, to attend the conference himself. Many did not think it was something he ought to be doing, bargaining in this fashion with envoys of the rebellion. He was as skeptical as anybody that any good would come from it, but it was a case of trying whatever might work.

On February 2 he wired Grant, who was making the commissioners comfortable on a Hudson River boat, the *Mary Martin*, anchored in Hampton Roads. "Say to the gentlemen," Lincoln instructed Grant, "that I will meet them personally at Fortress Monroe as soon as I can get there." At the same time, he advised Seward to stand by; he was on his way. Lincoln boarded the *Thomas Collyer*, a steamer designed for speed, and reached Hampton Roads a little after ten o'clock the night of February 2. There he boarded the *River Queen*, the presidential steamer, where Seward waited.[8]

Mary Chesnut in South Carolina was at least as skeptical as Lincoln. "And we have sent Stephens, Campbell—all who never believed in this thing—to negotiate for peace," she complained to her diary on January 17. "No hope—no good. Who dares hope?"[9] The prospect seemed to bear out Mary's pessimism. Each side was coming with demands unacceptable to the other. Lincoln was calling for one common country; Davis would not accept anything short of Confederate independence. But they were going to meet anyhow.

The commissioners boarded the *River Queen*, anchored about 275 yards from shore, the morning of February 3. In the steamer's saloon, where they were to meet, Lincoln watched in great amusement as Stephens, an old friend from their days together in the House of Representatives in the late 1840s, climbed out of his huge greatcoat. Stephens was a man with a giant's mind in a shrimp's body, who could not top a hundred pounds on a very heavy day. What came from the overcoat, Lincoln thought as he watched Stephens emerge from it, was "the biggest shuck and the littlest ear" that he ever did see.[10]

The five men—Lincoln, Seward, and the three Confederates—sat down for an informal talk that ran on for four hours. Nobody else was in the room, and no papers were exchanged. It was later described as "a long and rambling talk," entirely friendly and courteous, and producing what seemed foreordained: nothing.[11] Lincoln from the start reiterated his conditions: he could enter into no treaty, convention, stipulation, or agreement with the Confederate states, jointly or separately, about an armistice or any other subject without first reaching an agreement to restore the Union. Anything short of that, Lincoln said, "would be a quasi recognition of the states then in arms against the national government as a separate power." That he could never do.[12]

The Confederates, Seward later wrote, seemed to advocate a postponement of the question of separation to let passions cool, the armies scale down, and trade and intercourse resume. Lincoln viewed that idea as simply an armistice that could not get around his indispensable preconditions. Seward later wrote that Lincoln, when his conditions were met, would exercise every liberality not limited by the Constitution. So the conference ended without agreement of views on any of the matters discussed. Nonetheless, Seward believed, on the plus side, "we have been able to submit our opinions and views directly to prominent insurgents, and to hear them in answer in a courteous and not unfriendly manner."[13]

It was both the first and last meeting to try for a negotiated agreement to end the war—what might be fairly styled as "a peace conference."[14] It did not set any popularity records in the Confederacy. An official in the government called it "this peace *fiasco*," which left "nothing whatever to hope or expect short of the exaction of all the right of conquest, whether we are overrun by force, or submit."[15]

When Lincoln and Seward returned to Washington, an antsy Congress wanting to know what had been going on passed a resolution calling for a full report. Lincoln obliged with messages and documents spelling it all out from beginning to end.

And the war continued.

CHAPTER SEVEN

WITH MALICE TOWARD NONE

Back in Washington, Lincoln, with an end to the continuing war in sight, now prepared for a new beginning—his second term.

Henry Raymond was a multitasker, serving as both the editor of the *New York Times* and the Republican Party chairman. Lincoln called him "my lieutenant general in politics."[1] That noted editor-general believed that "the close of President Lincoln's first Administration was brilliant in itself, and gave full promise of yet brighter things to come." Like most in the North, Raymond saw that "the fierceness of the storm seemed to be passing away, and clearer skies to be seen through the rolling clouds."[2]

The electoral votes from the canvass in November had been counted, and Lincoln had been formally notified that he was reelected. He would be inaugurated on March 4, 1865. On March 1 he responded to the notification committee. "Having served four years in the depths of a great, and yet unended national peril," he wrote, "I can view this call to a second term, in nowise more flatteringly to myself, than as an expression of the public judgment, that I may better finish a difficult work, in which I have labored from the first, than could any one less severely schooled to the task." That said, Lincoln then ended his acceptance: "With assured reliance on that Almighty Ruler who has so graceously [*sic*] sustained us thus far; and with increased gratitude to the generous people for their continued confidence, I accept the renewed trust, with it's [*sic*] yet onerous and perplexing duties and responsibilities."[3]

The night before the inaugural had been stormy, cold, and wet. Wind and hail had battered the skylights of the Capitol. As day was breaking, a sudden violent burst hit with the fury of an explosion. Many weary members of the old Congress, winding up last-hour business before giving way to the new, rose from their seats and rushed for the door in alarm.[4] Rain continued in torrents, not abating until late morning and then giving way to a somber, bleak, drizzly day with gusting winds and clouds hanging low to the earth—a day of "tearful skies," as Noah Brooks put it.[5]

It had in fact been raining for two days throughout the East, and the streets of Washington were rivers of mud— mud, Brooks moaned, that "excelled all the other varieties I have ever seen before or since." Despite the mud, a vast concourse had begun gathering early around the inaugural platform erected on the east portico of the Capitol. Brooks pitied the ladies, "bedraggled and drenched" and "in most wretched, wretched plight; crinoline was smashed, skirts bedaubed, and moiré antique, velvet, laces and such were streaked with mud from end to end. Such another dirty crowd probably was never seen."[6]

Andrew Johnson of Tennessee, the new vice president elect, had not wanted to attend this seminal event. A Democrat, he had been the military governor of the loyal eastern end of his state, in the very furnace of the rebellion, throughout the war. Tennessee had seceded, and his job, being the military governor of its still-loyal, refuse-to-go-along eastern end, was perhaps the toughest and most disagreeable job in the country—like being behind enemy lines in a war zone.

Now a full-time governor and legislature were to be elected in the state on March 4, the day of the inaugural, and would meet on the first Monday in April to begin to resume all the functions of a state in the Union. Johnson wrote to Lincoln, "I would prefer remaining where I am until that time, and then hand it all over to the people."[7]

Lincoln would not hear of it. "While we [Lincoln and several cabinet members] fully appreciate your wish to remain in Tennessee until her State-Government shall be completely re-inaugerated [*sic*]," he wrote his vice president to be, "it is our unanimous conclusion that it is unsafe for you not to be here on the fourth of March. Be sure to reach here by that time."[8] A recent threat to the lives of Lincoln,

Seward, and Johnson had caused the president to fear for the safety of his new vice president in Tennessee.[9]

Johnson did reach Washington on time, but many in hindsight would wish he hadn't. He was inaugurated first, before Lincoln, not on the east portico before the gathering muddy masses, but in the Senate chamber. To the horror of everybody present, Johnson appeared to be drunk. He launched into a painfully prolonged, partly incoherent tirade, "remarkable," the *New York Herald* said, "only for its incoherence"[10]—not at all what was expected of a new vice president. After taking the oath of office on the Bible, he snatched up the Holy Book and, facing the audience, pronounced loudly, "I kiss this Book in the face of my nation of the United States"—which he then did, theatrically.[11]

If Johnson appeared drunk, it was for a reason. He had been ill and had taken liquor as a curative. But Johnson did not hold his liquor well, and that fact became mortifyingly and disgustingly apparent to his audience, which included Lincoln. This was no way to start an inaugural. But Lincoln, an ever-forgiving man, later said of the incident, "I have known Andy Johnson for many years. He made a bad slip the other day, but you need not be scared; Andy ain't a drunkard."[12]

Following Johnson's disreputable turn, about midday, suited all in black, Lincoln walked from the Senate chamber to the east portico to be inaugurated. Noah Brooks watched and described him as a "pathetic melancholy figure" rising "tall and gaunt, over the crowd about him."[13] "The tall form," the *New York Herald* wrote, "was in harmony with the scene, and its bold outline served only to distinguish him as the man above all others of that grand occasion."[14]

As Lincoln stepped forward to read his inaugural address, the sun broke briefly through the tearful clouds in an astonishing burst of light. Lincoln later said to Brooks, "Did you notice that sunburst? It made my heart jump."[15]

Before he started to speak, Lincoln paused, "as though thronging memories impeded utterance; then, in a voice clear and strong, but touched with pathos," he began reading his address.[16] His voice, one observer noted, was "singularly clear and penetrating" with "a sort of metallic ring."[17]

"Fellow Countrymen: At this second appearing to take the oath of the presidential office," he began, "there is less occasion for an extended address than there was at the first." Anyone who cared to count the words on the two broad columns on the half sheet of foolscap he was holding would have found but 703.

Lincoln continued, speaking of the first inaugural. "Then," he said, "a statement, somewhat in detail, of a course to be pursued, seemed fitting and proper. Now, at the expiration of four years, during which public declarations have been constantly called forth on every point and phase of the great contest which still absorbs the attention, and engrosses the enerergies [*sic*] of the nation, little that is new could be presented. The progress of our arms, upon which all else chiefly depends, is as well known to the public as to myself; and it is, I trust, reasonably satisfactory and encouraging to all. With high hope for the future, no prediction in regard to it is ventured."

Still lingering on the first inaugural, Lincoln then reminded the vast throng, "On the occasion corresponding to this four years ago, all thoughts were anxiously directed to an impending civil-war. All dreaded it—all sought to avert it. While the inaugeral [*sic*] address was being delivered from this place, devoted altogether to *saving* the Union without war, insurgent agents were in the city seeking to *destroy* it without war—seeking to dissol[v]e the Union, and divide effects, by negotiation. Both parties deprecated war; but one of them would *make* war rather than let the nation survive; and the other would *accept* war rather than let it perish. And the war came."

Lincoln made it clear why it had come. "One eighth of the whole population were colored slaves," he said, "not distributed generally over the Union, but localized in the Southern part of it. These slaves constituted a peculiar and powerful interest. All knew that this interest was, somehow, the cause of the war. To strengthen, perpetuate, and extend this interest was the object for which the insurgents would rend the Union, even by war; while the government claimed no right to do more than to restrict the territorial enlargement of it."

The president explained how it had not gone as anybody had imagined or as many had prayed it would. "Neither party," he went on, "expected for the war, the magnitude, or the duration, which it has already attained. Neither anticipated that the *cause* of the conflict might cease with, or even before, the conflict itself should cease. Each looked for an easier triumph, and a result less fundamental and astounding." Both, he said, "read the same Bible, and pray to the same God; and each invokes His aid against the other. It may seem strange that any men should dare to ask a just God's assistance in wringing their bread from the sweat of other men's faces; but let us judge not that we be not judged. The prayers of both could not be answered; that of neither has been answered fully."

Lincoln then pointed out that there was not much anybody could do about what God intends. "The Almighty," he went on, "has His own purposes." So who was to blame for all this? All of us, Lincoln in effect said. "'Woe unto the world because of offenses!'" he continued, quoting scripture, "'for it must needs be that offences come; but woe to that man by whom the offence cometh!' If we shall suppose that American Slavery is one of those offences which, in the providence of God, must needs come, but which, having continued through His appointed time, He now wills to remove, and that He gives to both North and South, this terrible war, as the woe due to those by whom the offence came, shall we discern therein any departure from those divine attributes which the believers in a Living God always ascribe to Him?"

So what can we expect? "Fondly do we hope—fervently do we pray—," Lincoln continued, "that this mighty scourge of war may speedily pass away. Yet, if God wills that it continue, until all the wealth piled by the bond-man's two hundred and fifty years of unrequited toil shall be sunk, and until every drop of blood drawn with the lash, shall be paid by another drawn with the sword, as was said three thousand years ago, so still it must be said 'the judgments of the Lord, are true and righteous altogether.'"

Lincoln had yet one more thing, very important on his mind, that must be said. The president was a close reader of Shakespeare and was familiar with the hymn of mercy spoken by Portia to Shylock, the Jew, in *The Merchant of Venice*:

Then must the Jew be merciful. . . .
The Quality of mercy is not strain'd,
It droppeth as the gentle rain from heaven
Upon the place beneath; it is twice bless'd;
It blesseth him that gives and him that takes:
'Tis mightiest in the mightiest; it becomes
The throned monarch better than his crown;
His scepter shows the force of temporal power;
The attribute to awe and majesty,
Wherein doth sit the dread and fear of kings;
But mercy is above the sceptred sway,
It is enthroned in the hearts of kings,
It is an attribute to God himself,
And earthly power doth then show likest God's
When mercy seasons justice.[18]

Scene of the second inaugural, where Lincoln spoke his immortal words of mercy: "With malice toward none; with charity for all." Courtesy of the Abraham Lincoln Presidential Library and Museum.

In the final words of his inaugural address, Lincoln was now about to contribute his own hymn of mercy: "With Malice toward none; with charity for all; with firmness in the right, as God gives us to see the right, let us strive on to finish the work we are in; to bind up the nation's wounds; to care for him who shall have borne the battle, and for his widow, and his orphan—to do all which may achieve and cherish a just, and a lasting peace, among ourselves, and with all nations."[19]

When the brief address ended, Chief Justice Chase swore Lincoln in. The Bible before him lay open to Isaiah 5, verses 27 and 28: "None shall be weary nor stumble among them; none shall slumber nor sleep; neither shall the girdle of their loins be loosed, nor the latchet of their shoes be broken: Whose arrows are sharp, and all their bows bent, their horses' hoofs shall be counted like flint, their wheels like a whirlwind."

They were verses that could have resonated with Lincoln—willing his people and his own armies, with victory so close at hand, not to be weary, nor slumber or sleep, not to let the figurative girdle of their loins be loosed or the latchet of their shoes be broken. He willed them, with sharp arrows, bent bows, hoofs like flint, and wheels like a whirlwind, to press implacably on to the imminent end.

Lincoln kissed the Bible and lifted his head to a celebratory salvo of artillery. Cheers rang out over the thunder of the cannons, and the newly reinaugurated president bowed to the people. His second term had begun. It was a hopeful day in another way as well: as Lincoln was inaugurated, the legislatures of seventeen of the thirty-four states—half of them—had ratified the Thirteenth Amendment. The "Sacred Book" that Lincoln had kissed, "the page marked that was touched by his lips," was sent to Mary Lincoln with a note from Chief Justice Chase.[20]

The 703 words of the inaugural address were words for the ages. Many recognized that immediately. George Templeton Strong, the insightful diarist in New York, said it was "unlike any American state paper of this century," most unlike "the inaugurals of Pierce, Polk, Buchanan, or any of their predecessors."[21] Charles Francis Adams Jr.

wrote to his father, the American minister in London, "This inaugural strikes me in its grand simplicity and directness as being for all time the historical keynote of this war. . . . Not a prince or minister in all Europe could have risen to such an equality with the occasion."[22]

William Gladstone, the British statesman, called it "unquestionably a most striking and sublime utterance, not surpassed by any delivered during the nineteenth century."[23] The London *Spectator* echoed Gladstone, calling the address "by far the noblest which any American President has yet uttered to an American Congress."[24] Frederick Douglass, the black abolitionist, often critical of Lincoln for not moving faster on emancipation, thought it "sounded more like a sermon than like a state paper." But when Lincoln, valuing Douglass's opinion, asked him directly what he thought of it at the postinaugural levee, Douglas said, "Mr. Lincoln, that was a sacred effort."[25]

There were critics, however, who did not consider it anything like a sacred effort—notably the Democratic press. The rabidly Democratic *Chicago Times*, a longtime bitter Lincoln enemy, asked, "Was there ever such a coming out of the little end of the horn?" The paper called the speech "slip shod," "loose-jointed," and "puerile." "By the side of it," the *Times* said, "mediocrity is superb. Let us trust in Heaven that it is not typical of our national degeneracy."[26]

Lincoln supplied his own take on the address in a letter to Thurlow Weed, the New York editor and Republican party wire-puller. "I expect [it] to wear as well as—perhaps better than—any thing I have produced," Lincoln wrote Weed, "but I believe it is not immediately popular. Men are not flattered by being shown that there has been a difference of purpose between the Almighty and them."[27]

Two days after the inaugural, on March 6, a gala ball was held at the spacious Patent Office, shimmering with decorations "of the richest character."[28] Lincoln invited Speaker of the House Schuyler Colfax and Senator Charles Sumner to accompany him and Mrs. Lincoln. Even Sumner, an untiring critic of Lincoln's benevolent reconstruction plans, had rather grudgingly conceded after the inaugural address, "We must all admit that he has said some things better than any body else could have said them."[29]

In the brilliantly lit ballroom of the Patent Office, Lincoln and Colfax led the line to the presidential platform. Mrs. Lincoln, wearing a white lace dress over a white silk skirt, her hair adorned in a wreath of white jessamines and purple violets, followed on Sumner's arm. It was an arrangement to meet Mrs. Lincoln's approval. Sumner was one of her favorites, a frequent visitor to the White House, and Lincoln was leading the procession, but not with another woman on his arm. Mrs. Lincoln would not have stood for that.

Noah Brooks stared at all the glitter and gushed, "Such another display of laces, jewelry, silks and feathers, gold lace and things was never seen, no, not since the world began."[30]

C H A P T E R   E I G H T

AT THE SEAT OF WAR

While Lincoln was discussing peace with Confederate commissioners in early February 1865 and urging malice toward none in early March, William Tecumseh Sherman was on a tear through the Carolinas that looked to Southerners little like peace and a lot like malice. Sherman had lingered in Savannah for more than a month finalizing plans to move on. His eye, which Confederates must have thought baleful, was now firmly fixed on the Carolinas, and he intended to make those two seedbeds of rebellion howl as he had made Georgia howl.

On February 1, under rare clear skies, he launched his juggernaut northward. Along the path to his destination—Goldsboro, North Carolina, 425 miles from Savannah and 145 from Petersburg—lay the two jewel cities of the rebellion, Columbia and Charleston in South Carolina. Both could expect powerful vengeance.

As Sherman's army moved out, the soldiers of each regiment raised three rousing cheers as they passed into South Carolina. At last, Union major general Henry Slocum later wrote, they had "set foot on the State which had done more than all others to bring upon the country the horrors of civil war."[1]

To try to slow these doomsday legions, the Confederates were rallying troops, many of them the broken fragments of Hood's shattered Army of Tennessee, who were being hurried over into Sherman's path. But if anything was likely to slow Sherman, it was not a Confederate army, but swampy terrain and angry skies. The Carolinas had become a bog, and the heavens wept almost without letup. The "sun grew dim," a Union officer wrote, and the rains came, drenching the days and making a "miry bivouac" of the nights.[2]

It was a "semi-amphibian" march over wretched roads of bottomless mud, flooded streams, and ill-mapped swamps—a quagmire that had to be overlaid with corduroy roads. It became a case, a Union general wrote, of "bridging chaos for hundreds of miles." The country, another officer wrote, was "one sheet of water." Even the mules, he said, "became discouraged." Slogging with Sherman through this Southern morass were thousands of black refugees and contrabands, continuing to follow the soldiers to freedom, seeming at times nearly equal in number to the army they were clinging to.[3]

The army marked some ten miles a day, even through the swamps, not yet meeting any effective organized resistance. "We have been able to brush them off our path like so many flies," one soldier described it. Sherman's men arrived on the banks of the Congaree River outside Columbia on February 17. As the army marched toward the city, a soldier began singing "John Brown's Body." Soon the song, carried by thirty thousand soldier voices, "rolled up and down the valley."[4]

Sherman led his horse over a newly laid pontoon bridge and onto a broad road leading into the town. "A high and boisterous wind was prevailing from the north," he later wrote, "and flakes of cotton were flying about in the air and lodging in the limbs of the trees, reminding us of a Northern snow-storm."[5]

That night Columbia burned. It is still unclear and a point of contention who started the fire. Southerners blamed Sherman's soldiers, who wound up fighting it. Sherman denied that, insisting the fire was started by the Confederates themselves. However it started, Emma Florence LeConte, the sixteen-year-old daughter of a professor at the state university at Columbia, wrote in her journal that it was an inferno that turned night into noonday. A "palpitating blaze," she said, walled the streets "with solid masses of flames as far as the eye could reach—filling the air with its terrible roar." On every side was "crackling and devouring fire" and "the crashing of timber and the thunder of falling buildings." A "quivering molten ocean" seemed to fill a "copper colored sky," across which rolled columns of black smoke "glittering with sparks and flying embers."[6] The next morning, Sherman recalled, "rose bright and clear over a ruined city," half of it "in ashes and smouldering heaps."[7]

That same morning the Confederates abandoned Charleston, deserting it to escape almost certain capture by Union columns "folding in around them like a constrictor around its prey."[8] The wail of despair in the South was profound. "A dark day, truly!" a young rebel war clerk in Richmond mourned in his diary. "Poor South Carolina! her day of agony has come!" That morning in Richmond was "as lovely a morning as ever dawned on earth. A gentle southern breeze, a cloudless sky, and a glorious morning sun." But "how dark and dismal the aspect of our military affairs!"[9] George Templeton Strong, the diarist in New York, read reprints of editorials in Southern newspapers and wrote, "Their sound is as the dying howl of a suppressed ram-cat with a shattered spine."[10]

Mary Chesnut had fled Columbia as the sound of Sherman's bugles neared, retreating to Lincolnton, in remote southwest North Carolina, "a thoroughly out-of-all routes place." There she was, she told her diary, "brokenhearted—an exile." As Sherman left Columbia and Charleston and continued thundering northward in yet more pounding rain, she cried, "Heaven is helping us weep. Rain, rain, rain—in sympathy with our calamities." Our world, she wrote, "has gone to destruction."[11]

The woe deepened when Confederate forces still holding Wilmington abandoned that city on February 21—for much the same reason they had abandoned Charleston. Union soldiers, twenty thousand from George Thomas's western army under John Schofield's command, marched in the next day, George Washington's birthday.

But trouble now lay ahead. A thirty-thousand-man Confederate force had been patched together, augmented by the flotsam from Hood's shattered army, with General Joseph E. Johnston newly in command. It was hovering nearby, about to challenge the march. Nobody knew the odds against success better than Johnston. He had made up his mind that there had been no such army as Sherman's "since the days of Julius Caesar."[12] But he attacked anyway on the still, balmy Sunday morning of March 19 in Bentonville, North Carolina. The most he could hope for was to slow Sherman's advance.

Sherman muscled him aside in a fierce, sharp two-day fight and, four days later, on March 23, rode into Goldsboro, the end of the march, at the head of his triumphant army. There he would soon be joined by Schofield with his twenty thousand veterans.

In Goldsboro, Sherman summarized what it had all meant. "Thus was concluded," he wrote in his memoirs, "one of the longest and most important marches ever made by an organized army in a civilized country"—425 miles from Savannah to Goldsboro.[13] One of his officers exulted, "We have now marched a great army diagonally across and through the very heart of the first and most bitter and obstinate of all the rebel states . . . sweeping everything before us."[14]

Sherman's march from Atlanta to Goldsboro, a reporter wrote, had assumed "the aspect of a great swinging movement, the pivot of which was the army before Petersburg." This monumental swing, "described on a radius of half a continent," was "one of those colossal enterprises whereof there are few exemplars in military history, and which fill up the measure of the imagination with the shapes of all that is vast and grandiose in war."[15] Somebody had once said of Sherman that his brain was "a splendid piece of machinery with all the screws loose." There had been nothing loose about his screws in his epic march through Georgia and the Carolinas, however.[16]

At Columbia, an old black woman had said to Sherman, "Bress de Lord, yer will hab a place in heaben; yer will go dar, sure." Sherman was content just getting as far as Goldsboro. "When I once plant this army at Goldsboro," he had said, "Lee must leave Virginia, or he will be defeated beyond hope of recovery."[17] That, of course, had been Sherman's whole purpose all along—to draw "from the mountains to the sea a wall of bayonets that imprisoned the enemy between himself and the Army of the Potomac."[18] Now in Goldsboro, he and Grant were "in position to catch Lee between [their] two thumbs."[19] Indeed, Lee seemed caught "on the horns of two dilemmas," with Sherman and Major General Phil Sheridan closing in on his communications from two directions, and Grant "holding him fast before Richmond."[20]

Everywhere now were "the omens of doom" for the Confederacy.[21] Abraham Lincoln was seeing that as clearly as anybody. Addressing the 140th Indiana Regiment on March 17, he noted "the recent effort of our erring bretheren [*sic*] . . . to employ the slaves in their armies." The desperate Confederacy was gearing up to do that, and to Lincoln it was a telling sign. He told the soldiers, "We have to reach the bottom of the insurgent resources; and that they employ, or seriously think of employing, the slaves as soldiers, gives us glimpses of the bottom."[22]

Lincoln was making ready the procedures to pursue when the Confederates truly reached that bottom. In early March he was telling Grant clearly what the general must and must not do as the end drew near. On March 3 Secretary of War Stanton, speaking for Lincoln, wired Grant, "The President directs me to say to you that he wishes you to have no conference with General Lee unless it be for the capitulation of Gen. Lee's army, or on some minor, and purely, military matter. He instructs me to say that you are not to decide, discuss, or confer upon any political question. Such questions the President holds in his own hands. . . . Meantime you are to press to the utmost, your military advantages."[23]

The long war, about to end, with perhaps one more campaign to be waged and won, had nonetheless left its sad mark on Lincoln. His face, one observer said, looked "care-ploughed, tempest-tossed and weatherbeaten."[24] He had been feeling physically unwell. His Illinois friend Orville Browning visited him in late February and found him looking bad and feeling down. Browning described Lincoln as "apparently more depressed than I have seen him since he became President."[25]

But on March 20 Grant sent Lincoln a mood-cheering invitation. "Can you not visit City Point for a day or two?" Grant asked. "I would like very much to see you and I think the rest would do you good." Lincoln leaped to accept. "Your kind invitation received," he wired Grant. "Had already thought of going immediately after the next rain. Will go sooner if any reason for it. Mrs. L. and a few others will probably accompany me." On the twenty-third Lincoln wired Grant, "We start to you at One P.M. to-day. May lie over during the dark hours of the night. Very small party of us." Going with him were Mary, her maid, and eleven-year-old Tad, about to become twelve. Stanton also sent William H. Crook and Captain Charles B. Penrose to accompany the president.[26]

They left aboard the *River Queen*, Lincoln's seagoing White House, escorted by the side-wheeling steamer USS *Bat*, a dispatch boat operating out of Washington and commanded by Lieutenant Commander John S. Barnes. The *Bat* was a captured blockade runner, long, narrow, and swift. It was built to run, capable of nineteen knots, but for this occasion it was throttled down to run with the president in the *River Queen*.

The two vessels were escorted out of Washington by a furious gale. In the capital as they left, the tempest was uprooting trees, unroofing houses, and wrecking a vessel at the Sixth Street wharf. Lincoln was escaping to the seat of war in this howling wind, an officer thought, with the "sad face" of "one whose heart was sick with hope deferred." But this time the omens suggested something different—that the hope might not be deferred much longer, that this time the end was truly in sight.[27]

The party docked at nine o'clock the next night, March 24, at City Point, and Grant came on board to welcome them. Early the next day Lincoln plunged into the mix. Nearly every morning after breakfast, a tug carried him to City Point. This war had a way of changing sleepy little hamlets few had ever visited or even heard of into benchmarks of history. Of no out-of-the-way hamlet was this truer than City Point. Before the war, it was a little Virginia town drowsing on the riverbank where the Appomattox empties into the James. But during the war, it had become what one historian much later called "one of the world's great seaports," perhaps the greatest staging ground for war in history. "Wharves lined the waterfront for more than a mile," the historian wrote, "with more docks extending up the Appomattox. An average day would see 40 steamboats, 75 sailing vessels, and 100 barges tied up or anchored along the waterfront."[28] As these overwhelming numbers suggest, the little hamlet had become, by a twist of history, one vast military metroplex.

Into it Lincoln dived daily, going directly to the adjutant's office to get the latest overnight news from the front, often then conferring with Grant and other officers. He threw himself eagerly into the action of the closing days. He told stories and joined in the laughter as enthusiastically as his listeners. The army seemed as happy to have him there as he was to be there.[29]

It had been a hard winter. Snow had fallen ten different times. Rain fell, moderately to heavily, on forty-three different days. Now it was March. The weather had turned fair, the roads were drying, and Grant was uneasy. He was not worried that the war would not end in victory. It was said that he "felt as sure of capturing Richmond as he did of dying."[30] He was worried about what the cagey Robert E. Lee might be thinking of doing.

Stalled before Petersburg through the fall and winter, Grant was anxious to launch a major push to end the war before Lee did anything. The hard winter was mellowing into a soft spring. Grant was waiting now only for an end to the abnormally heavy rains and the arrival of General Sheridan and his nine-thousand-man cavalry from the Shenandoah Valley. Grant had in mind to use Sheridan as the point of his dagger to end it all. But as he waited, Grant later wrote, "I was afraid, every morning, that I would awake from my sleep to hear that Lee had gone, and that nothing was left but a picket line," that "we would have the same army to fight again farther south—and the war might be prolonged another year."[31]

By March 24, the day Lincoln arrived for his visit to the army, the roads had dried and Sheridan had arrived. "I mean to end this business here," Grant said.[32] He ordered a general movement of his army operating against Richmond—a last mighty push—for March 29. Sheridan with his cavalry command was to strike the Confederate right and rear, causing Lee to shift forces there and weaken his middle, which Grant would then strike. Sherman was to cut off any rebel retreat in the direction of Danville should the main army break through at Petersburg and force Lee out of his entrenchments.

Grant's nightmare that Lee might bolt and make a run to unite with Johnston in North Carolina before he could strike this war-ending blow was well founded. Even as Grant on March 24 issued his order for a general movement, Lee was about to try, the next morning, to do what Grant feared—crash the Union line and break out. His target was a point on the line guarded by a nine-month-old Union rampart called Fort Stedman—one of the weakest redoubts in the thirty-mile-long federal front.

The fort was a square, enclosed Union bulwark covering an acre of ground in a grove of trees on the far Union right of the siege line. Close by, virtually a part of Stedman, was Battery 10, bristling with mortars, a small earthwork without bastions but with flanking batteries.

At no other time in the war had the two armies lain so close for so long than at the siege of Petersburg in the fall and winter of 1864–65. "Never before during the season when earth and sky placed an embargo on campaigning in Virginia," a Union officer wrote, "had the hostile forces been so near to each other. So close was the contact that we could almost feel the pulse and hear the breathing of the hostile army."[33] At no other point, perhaps, were the thirty miles of trench line closer than at Fort Stedman, where, a Confederate general said, it was "almost certain death for a man to show his head above the works on the front line."[34]

Grant, so long stalled before Petersburg, said, "I mean to end this business here." Courtesy of the National Archives, photograph no. 111-B-36.

Lee saw in Fort Stedman his best chance to smash through and open an escape hatch to Danville. His situation was bordering on desperate. His army was being shredded daily by desertions, wholesale, by the hundreds—of men who were hungry, tired of fighting, demoralized by impending defeat, needed at home. Deserters were flowing into Washington in a flood—as many as 150 a day—"tired of fighting for rich men's niggers" and ready to take oaths of allegiance to the national government. One of them told Noah Brooks, "You folks needn't have to fight with Old Bob Lee. Just hold on and worry him, as you are doing now, and he ain't going to have anything to fight with."[35]

Lee's idea as he considered Fort Stedman was to break the Union line there and push on through to the military railroad less than two miles beyond. From there he would make a run to unite with Johnston's army in Carolina before Grant could organize a pursuit.

The signal for the attack was to be three musket or pistol shots in quick succession. They came in the moonless predawn hours on March 25, a cold but clear Annunciation Day. The lead Confederate storming party surged across the federal line. The force of the attack briefly overran the fort and two nearby batteries. But it was a short-lived victory, a hope unfulfilled. A strong Union countercharge drove the Confederates back by midmorning. Lee's planned escape gambit was at an end.

Lincoln had been less than five miles from the action, and in the afternoon he visited the scene of the battle, where bloodied bodies still lay on the ground. He said, sadly, "that he had seen enough of the horrors of war, that he hoped this was the beginning of the end and that there would be no more bloodshed or ruin of homes."[36]

That appeared a forlorn hope. The attack did nothing to change Grant's order for a rebellion-killing movement on March 29. It was likely to bring an end to the war, but not to the bloodshed and the ruin of homes.

C H A P T E R N I N E

"THIS MEANS VICTORY"

At three in the morning on March 29 Grant launched the movement he had ordered on the twenty-fourth. It had all the trappings and expectations of a final campaign—and doom for Lee's army. At nine o'clock Grant and his staff rode off for the front, leaving Lincoln in City Point but not out of the loop. The president would be immediately updated on the progress of the fighting.

Grant liked and appreciated Lincoln. "The President," he said, "is one of the few visitors I have had who has not attempted to extract from me a knowledge of my plans. He not only never asked them, but says it is better he should not know them, and then he can be certain to keep the secret." Grant understood how Lincoln felt while awaiting news from the front: "He will be the most anxious man in the country to hear from us, his heart is so wrapped up in our success, but I think we can send him some good news in a day or two."[1]

The campaign opened as so many others had in this war—under pouring rain. The skies had clouded during the day on March 29, and toward evening the rain started to fall, pouring down in torrents through the night and all the next day with little letup. The densely wooded country was drenched. Horace Porter of Grant's staff wrote, "It seemed as if the bottom had fallen out of the roads," turning them into "sheets of water" undergirded by mud. Horses were sinking to their bellies in "beds of quicksand," and wagons were at risk "to disappear altogether." It looked to Porter "as if the saving of that army would require the services, not of a Grant, but of a Noah."[2]

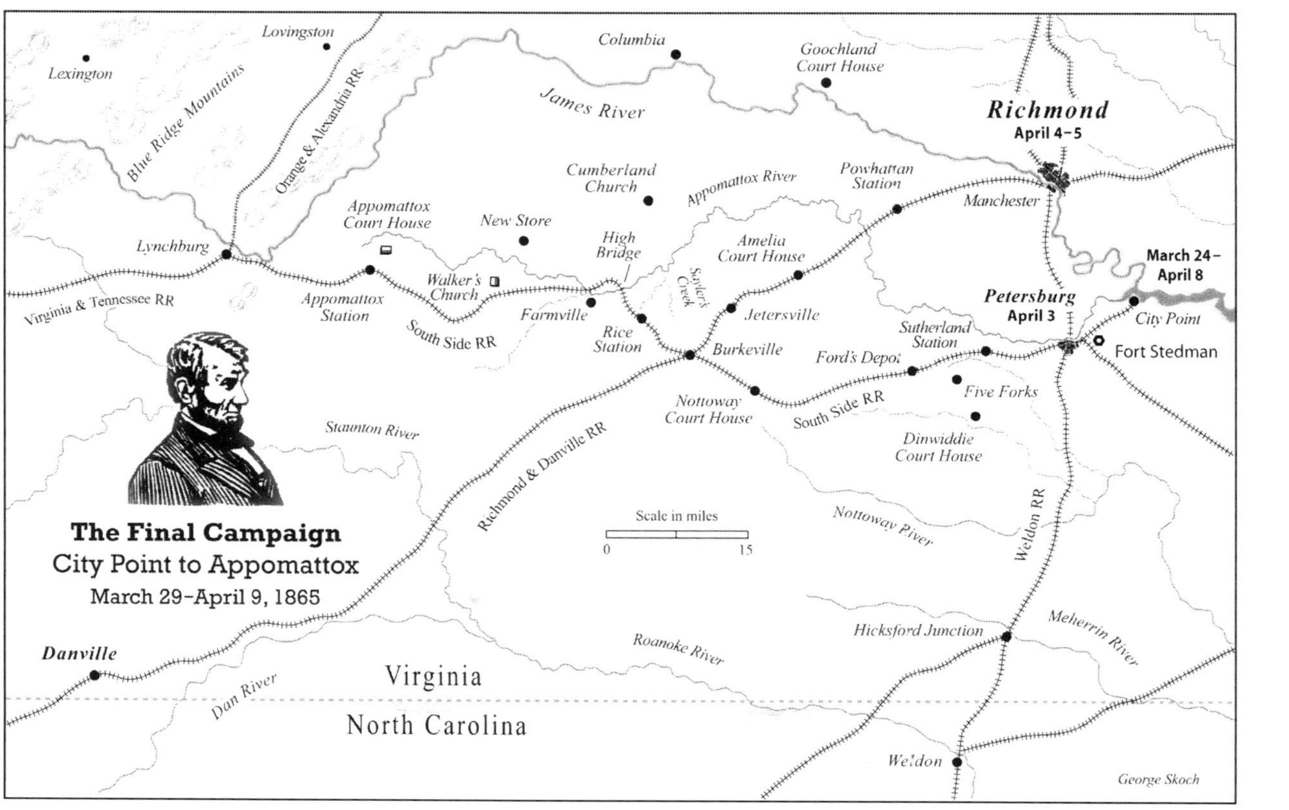

The Final Campaign
City Point to Appomattox
March 29–April 9, 1865
Lexington
Lovingston
Blue Ridge Mountains
Orange & Alexandria RR
Columbia
James River
Goochland Court House
Richmond
April 4–5
Cumberland Church
Appomattox River
Powhattan Station
Manchester
Appomattox Court House
New Store
High Bridge
Amelia Court House
Lynchburg
Walker's Church
Sayler's Creek
March 24–April 8
Virginia & Tennessee RR
Appomattox Station
Farmville
Jetersville
Petersburg
April 3
City Point
South Side RR
Rice Station
Burkeville
Sutherland Station
Fort Stedman
Ford's Depot
Five Forks
Nottoway Court House
South Side RR
Staunton River
Richmond & Danville RR
Dinwiddie Court House
Scale in miles
0
15
Nottoway River
Weldon RR
Hicksford Junction
Meherrin River
Roanoke River
Danville
Dan River
Virginia
North Carolina
Weldon
George Skoch

The deluge lifted the morning of March 31 and left the day cloudy and dismal. Grant went on the offensive under the frowning sky, hurling his spear—Sheridan's cavalry—as planned, at Lee's extreme right. All siege long, Grant had been inching his way toward Lee's right, hoping eventually to get around it. Now was the time for the coup de main, and Grant had his tool.

Sheridan was a bantam rooster in a human configuration. He was called "Little Phil" because he stood "scarce five feet high, with his sun-browned face and sailor air."[3] Ready to "go to smashing things,"[4] he was thundering on the first day of April toward Five Forks, a key crossroads on Lee's extreme right, twelve miles southwest of Petersburg. The day was foggy, the trees and leaves dripping and the fields still water soaked. At Five Forks, as his musicians, mounted on uniform gray horses, were blaring "Nellie Bly," Sheridan struck. It could not have been more devastating for Lee, a smashing blow that shattered his right flank.[5] A Union officer called it "the Waterloo of the Confederacy."[6] That night Grant, on cue, ordered the assault on the center of the Petersburg line for the next morning, April 2. Things were moving rapidly, as Grant had hoped. Forced evacuation and hurried flight had now become Lee's only options.

Lincoln read a late-night wire sent April 1 from Grant to one of his officers: "I have just heard from Sheridan. He has carried everything before him. . . . He has captured three brigades of infantry and a train of wagons and is now pushing up his success."[7] Grant sent Lincoln several Confederate battle flags captured at Five Forks. Lincoln seized them, unfurled them one by one, and burst out, "Here is something material—something I can see, feel, and understand. This means victory. This *is* victory."[8]

His lines broken in three places, Lee sent a message to that other president, Jefferson Davis, in Richmond on Sunday morning, April 2, informing him that both Petersburg and Richmond must be abandoned. Lee marched his army out of Petersburg that night. Flight and pursuit had begun, with Lee intent on departing his now untenable position on the James and heading up the Appomattox toward Danville. From there he would attempt the junction with Johnston's

Sheridan, known as "Little Phil," who was ready to "go to smashing things." Courtesy of the National Archives, photograph no. 111-BA-1570.

army. Sheridan was racing to head him off. It was now apparent that the campaign was "to be won by legs."[9]

Grant continued to keep Lincoln informed. Anxious from the start, as Grant had predicted he would be, Lincoln was firing off telegrams of his own. On March 29, the first day of the campaign, he wired Grant, "How do things look now?" That same day he inquired of Major General Godfrey Weitzel, whose force from the Army of the James was standing before Richmond, "What, if any thing, have you observed on your front to-day?"[10]

Lincoln was also keeping Secretary of War Stanton and Secretary of State Seward informed in Washington. "I begin to feel that I ought to be at home," he wired Stanton on March 30, "and yet I dislike to leave without seeing nearer to the end of General Grant's present movement." Stanton wired back the next day, urging him to remain: "I hope you will stay to see it out, or for a few days at least.

I have strong faith that your presence will have great influence . . . ; compared to that no other duty can weigh a feather. . . . A pause by the army now would do harm; if you are on the ground there will be no pause. All well here." When Mary Lincoln started home to Washington on April 1, Lincoln began updating her, telling her, "All now looks highly favorable."[11]

It had been a less than happy visit to the army for Mrs. Lincoln. She had insisted on accompanying her husband to City Point, viewing it as an opportunity to bring Tad, see Robert, and make it something of a family outing. By March 25, the day after they arrived, it turned sour. With heavy fighting expected to begin on March 29, all wives had been ordered to the rear—with the exception, Mrs. Lincoln learned, of the wife of Major General Charles Griffin, who had been granted a presidential dispensation to remain at the front. This suggested to Mrs. Lincoln that to get the dispensation, Mrs. Griffin must have seen the president alone.

Mrs. Lincoln had a strong jealous streak when it came to her husband. "Do you know," she raged at Adam Badeau of Grant's staff, "that I never allow the President to see any woman alone?" She was still simmering when, at a review of the troops the next day, she learned that Major General Edward O. C. Ord's wife, a particularly handsome and skilled horsewoman, had ridden alongside Lincoln on the way to the parade grounds. Boiling over with rage, she laid a furious tongue-lashing on Mrs. Ord so abusive that the young woman burst into tears. Mrs. Lincoln then repeatedly assailed her husband in the presence of officers on account of the two wives, which Lincoln bore, Badeau later wrote, "as Christ might have done."

For the next three days Mrs. Lincoln remained "indisposed" in her cabin aboard the *River Queen*. Now, on the first day of April, she was returning to Washington, and Lincoln was trying to keep her in the loop. Nothing further was said of the unhappy events at City Point.[12]

On the morning of April 2 Lincoln advised Stanton, "Dispatches frequently coming in. All going finely." He told his secretary of war that the line from the Appomattox River to Hatcher's Run had been broken, and forts, guns, and prisoners had been taken. Sheridan's cavalry was on the enemy's flank in the west, and the rails on the

South Side Railroad, the most important source of supply for Lee's army, were being ripped up. In the afternoon he forwarded Grant's latest wire to Stanton. "Everything has been carried from the left of the Ninth Corps," Grant reported. "The Sixth Corps alone captured more than 3,000 prisoners. The Second and Twenty-fourth Corps both captured forts, guns, and prisoners from the enemy. . . . We are now closing around the works of the line immediately enveloping Petersburg. All looks remarkably well."[13]

From evacuated Petersburg, Grant wired Lincoln on April 2 inviting the president to join him there. An exuberant Lincoln wired back, "Allow me to tender you, and all with you, the nations [*sic*] grateful thanks for this additional, and magnificent success. At your suggestion, I think I will visit you to-morrow."[14]

Early the next morning Grant awaited the president on the piazza of a deserted brick house at 21 Market Street in Petersburg. Lincoln strode through the gate with long, rapid strides, his face beaming with delight, and told Grant, "Do you know, general, that I have had a sort of a sneaking idea for some days that you intended to do something like this."[15] The two men talked for an hour and a half, then Lincoln started off on horseback for City Point.

Grant and his staff mounted their horses and hurried after the westward-moving army, now several miles in advance. As Grant rode, a message sent by General Weitzel overtook him with stunning news: Richmond had also fallen. Weitzel had taken possession that morning at about quarter after eight.

CHAPTER TEN

SITTING IN DAVIS'S SEAT

Spring at its most enchanting had come to Richmond. "The young leaves," the rebel Constance Cary wrote in a letter to her mother and brother, "are just shaking out, the fruit trees a mass of blossoms—the grass vividly green, the air nectar."[1]

Sunday morning, April 2, 1865, was particularly enchanting. Confederate colonel Alexander R. Boteler, who was in Richmond, saw it as "a lovely morning—such as makes one glad to be alive. A few floating vapors, interfused with light, softened the rays of the sun and the atmosphere, refreshed by recent rains, was filled with the fragrance of the early flowers of Spring. The streets were unusually silent, and the city, in its 'Sunday solitude,' seemed to be reposing in the holy calm of peaceful security. 'There was a Sabbath stillness in the air.'"[2] Church bells, the *Washington Evening Whig* wrote, "rang as usual, with nothing of alarm in their tone, and worshippers were as prompt and devout as was their wont."[3]

Jefferson Davis was in St. Paul's Episcopal Church in Richmond on this quiet, picture-perfect Sabbath morning when Lee's urgent message reached him that the lines in Petersburg had been broken and Richmond must be evacuated. The day quickly became unholy. Davis quietly left the church, and when the news of the broken lines became generally known, Richmond erupted in panic. Davis and other high Confederate officials hurried to pack up important government records and leave town. The rest of Richmond's population wanting out scrambled frantically for wagons, carriages, and other transportation.

Davis's countenance, one observer noted, was "haggard and care-worn," and his spirits were "greatly depressed" as he boarded the train for Danville that night.[4] When the war came, five rail lines had snaked into Richmond. Now only one promised escape—the track from Richmond to Danville. It was on that line that Davis and other high-level Confederates left the city that night. Constance Cary later wrote, "By nightfall all the flitting shadows of a Lost Cause had passed away under a heaven studded by bright stars."[5]

When Davis left, the Confederate government became what the New York diarist George Templeton Strong called "nomadic," with its "seat of government" probably resting "on the saddle which Jeff Davis bestrides." Strong envisaged Davis like the missing massa in Henry C. Work's song "The Year of Jubilo" ("Kingdom Coming"):

> He saw the smoke 'way down the ribber, where the
> Linkum gunboats lay,
> And he picked up his hat, and he left bery sudden,
> An I 'spec he's run away![6]

Davis did not run away, however, without hurling a Parthian shot of hope and defiance. From Danville, he exhorted the Confederate people, calling it "unwise and unworthy of us, as patriots engaged in a most sacred cause, to allow our energies to falter, our spirits to grow faint, or our efforts to become relaxed under reverses, however calamitous." He vowed, "It is my purpose to maintain your cause with my whole heart and soul." And he urged his fellow Confederates to "meet the foe with fresh defiance, with unconquered and unconquerable hearts," and with "unquenchable resolve," as he intended to do.[7]

But in the wake of his going, Richmond, deserted by authority, civil or military, was plunged into virtually unquenchable chaos—a "saturnalia," the *Washington Evening Whig* wrote; a "carnival of ruin," one Union officer called it.[8] Fire had broken out everywhere. By nightfall the city was being consumed, Alexander Boteler said, by "a fearful conflagration, which was made more terrible by the excesses of a drunken mob of plunderers, who were as fierce, as pitiless, and as unrestrained as the destroying flames around them." Vast volumes of lurid smoke rolled in billowy clouds across the crimson sky, "blotting out the stars." Above the "sullen roar of the flames," which sounded to Boteler like "the monotone of the surf upon a rocky shore, were heard at frequent intervals the crash of falling timbers accompanied with such yells and shrieks as made a very midnight pandemonium."[9]

Richmond was "like a blaze of day amid the surrounding darkness," another Confederate officer still in the city described it. Exploding incendiaries, or fragments of bombs from arsenals in the capital, had set buildings ablaze. "Every now and then," the officer wrote, "as a magazine exploded, a column of white smoke rose up as high as the eye could reach, instantaneously followed by a deafening sound. The earth seemed to rock and tremble as with the shock of an earthquake." The "immense magazines of exploding cartridges ignited the rattle as of thousands of musketry." At dawn unfinished ironclads down the river exploded with a thunderous roar.[10]

"The whole city," a Union officer later wrote, "jarred and vibrated with horrid sounds." Warehouses, stores, mills, bridges, depots, and dwellings collapsed. Loaded shells in the arsenals exploded in the heat, tearing through houses, plowing up streets and gardens, carrying with them death and destruction. Fire leaped "from building to building, from street to street," filling the city "with its scorching breath." By daylight on April 3 the plundering—worsening after convicts were let out of the penitentiary—had reached the vast commissary depot at Fourteenth and Cary Streets. Whiskey ran in the gutters and "rolled like a river of death rapidly on into the sewers," creating "a miniature whisky Niagara."[11]

As the new day dawned, yet another misery was clearly visible and distinctly heard across Richmond's seven hills. Union soldiers from the Army of the James were entering the city. A black regimental band marching in played the Confederate anthem, "Dixie."[12] As the Union troops drew near, Richmond mayor Joseph Mayo went out to meet them to formally surrender his city. Turning onto Main Street and headed for Capitol Square, the bands of the occupying army broke into the Union standards "Yankee Doodle," "Rally 'round the Flag," and "Battle Cry of Freedom."[13] As General Weitzel entered, he found Richmond "in a perfect pandemonium," with fires and explosions in all directions, the streets filled with "a yelling, howling mob." He ordered his staff to scour the city and press into service every able-bodied man, white or black, to fight and extinguish the fires.[14]

No telegraph wires had yet reached Richmond, so Weitzel sent a cavalry courier galloping to find a way to tell Grant, en route to join his army, that at long last the Confederate capital was in Union hands. It had taken four years of bloody fratricidal war for it to happen. It had been, one Union officer said, "the longest and hardest road an army ever traveled."[15]

When the news relayed from Grant reached Lincoln, the president said, "Thank God that I have lived to see this! It seems to me that I have been dreaming a horrid dream for four years, and now the nightmare is gone."[16] As Lincoln exulted, Constance Cary wept. "I have cried until no more tears will come," she wrote her mother and brother, "and my heart throbs to bursting night and day." To her Richmond "wore the aspect of [a town] in the Middle Ages smitten by pestilence." She wailed, "It is no longer our Richmond."[17]

Lincoln had a longing. He told Rear Admiral David Dixon Porter on April 3, "I want to see Richmond."[18] At five in the afternoon he wired Stanton, "I have already been to Petersburg. Staid with General Grant an hour and a half and returned here [to City Point]. It is certain now that Richmond is in our hands, and I think I will go there to-morrow." This presidential intention was chilling news to Stanton. He had worried enough over Lincoln's visit to captured Petersburg that morning. "Commanding generals," Stanton had admonished him, "are in the line of their duty in running such risks; but is the political head of a nation in the same condition?" Lincoln assured him, "I will take care of myself."[19]

Richmond's fall electrified Washington and ignited mutiple celebratory cannon salutes. The night of April 4, following the news, the capital erupted "in a tumult of Joy." Noah Brooks reported that both the private and public buildings were "all alight with rockets, fireworks and illuminations of every description." The streets were "one blaze of glory." A longtime Washingtonian wrote in his journal, "*All Washington* was in the streets. I never saw such a crowd out-of-doors in my life, that I remember—and I have seen immense crowds in my day." The visiting French count Charles de Chambrun found Senator Charles Sumner with "his cheeks wet with tears."

The general celebration was not all that dry either. Chambrun noted that whiskey, "a liquor horribly popular" that "contributes largely to the expression of the citizen's joy" in America, was in full flow—however, not into the gutters as in Richmond. "The day of jubilee did not end with the nightfall," Brooks wrote, but was prolonged far into the night, and "a more liquorish crowd was never seen in Washington." When the news reached Mary Lincoln, she exclaimed, "This is almost too much happiness, to be realized!"[20]

The *Chicago Journal* resorted to verse:

> What joyous tumult none may drown
> Is heard in every Northern town!
> What clamor rises, wild and free,
> And fills the land from sea to sea!
> What countless banners deck the sky
> All hearts are glad, all hopes are high
> For Union men march up and down
> The haughty streets of Richmond town![21]

On the morning of April 4, as Washington was gearing up to celebrate in a big way, it was mild and virtually windless on the James River. A small flotilla set off from City Point headed for Richmond, with Lincoln on the *River Queen*, escorted by the *Bat*, and Admiral Porter on his flagship, the *Malvern*. The transport *Columbus*, carrying a small cavalry escort and ambulances, and a tug to carry Lincoln to and from the *River Queen* completed the modest fleet.

Perhaps the most excited passenger on any of these vessels was Tad, Lincoln's young son, accompanying his father. He had more than one reason to be excited. He was going to visit fallen Richmond, and that day he was turning twelve years old.

An obstruction on the river beyond Drewry's Bluff caused Lincoln to be transferred to Porter's twelve-oar barge, rowed by a dozen sailors. This dramatic downsizing of the fleet carrying him to Richmond suggested a story to Lincoln—a not unusual thing with this president. "Brings to mind," Lincoln said, "a fellow who once came to me to ask for an appointment as minister abroad. Finding he could not get that, he came down to some more modest position. Finally he asked to be made a tide-waiter. When he saw he could not get that, he asked me for an old pair of trousers. But it is well to be humble."[22]

The barge, analogous to the old pair of trousers, took Lincoln the rest of the way. Because of the risk of torpedoes in the water, it landed on the riverbank just above Libby Prison, the three-story warehouse that had been the notorious bastille for captured Union officers, at about nine o'clock in the morning.

General Weitzel had been informed that Lincoln was coming, but the president had arrived sooner than expected. No officer, wagon, or escort was there to meet him. Sailors from the barge, armed with carbines, formed a guard around Lincoln, Tad, and the party—Admiral Porter, Captain Charles B. Penrose, Navy captain A. H. Adams, and Lieutenant W. W. Clemens of the Signal Corps. All on foot, they started to walk in the direction of the center of Richmond, about a mile and a half away. Much of the city was still on fire, and

Lincoln and Tad walking the streets of Richmond. The former slaves shouted, "President Linkum hab come! President Linkum hab come!" Courtesy of the National Portrait Gallery, Smithsonian Institution; Alan and Lois Fern Acquisition Fund.

their path led through charred ruins. All of this seemed foolhardy to Penrose, who later confessed that he had never in his life passed "a more anxious time than in this walk."[23]

When the party landed, as Porter later described it, the leader of a dozen black workers digging with spades raised himself upright and shielded his eyes to look. Then, dropping his spade and springing forward, the old man shouted, "Bress de Lord, dere is de great Messiah! I knowed him as soon as I seed him. He's bin in my heart fo' long yeahs, an' he's cum at las' to free his chillun from deir bondage! Glory, Hallelujah!"

Almost instantly, Porter testified, Lincoln was surrounded. Within moments the streets filled with former slaves. "They seemed to spring from the earth. They came, tumbling and shouting, from over the hills and from the water-side." Describing their jubilation, he said, "They all had their souls in their eyes, and I don't think I ever looked upon a scene where there were so many passionately happy faces."[24]

The party continued walking toward Richmond, escorted by the exultant black throng. The reporter Charles Coffin, who had arrived earlier in Richmond, watched as they edged along. He said to a black woman:

> "There is the man who made you free."
> "What, massa?"
> "That is President Lincoln."
> "Dat President Linkum?"
> "Yes."
> She gazed at him a moment in amazement, joy, rapture, as if in supernal presence, then clapped her hands, jumped and shouted, "Glory! glory! glory!" . . .
> "Hurrah! Hurrah! President Linkum hab come! President Linkum hab come!" rang through the street.
> . . . It was not a hurrah that they gave, so much as a wild, jubilant cry of inexpressible joy.
>
> They pressed around the President, ran ahead, and hovered upon the flanks and rear of the little company. Men, women, and children joined the constantly increasing throng. They

> came from all the streets, running in breathless haste, shouting and hallooing, and dancing with delight. The men threw up their hats, the women waved their bonnets and handkerchiefs, clapped their hands, and shouted, "Glory to God! glory! glory! glory!"[25]

A correspondent from the *Boston Journal*, thoroughly moved by this remarkable, unprecedented scene, wrote of Lincoln, "He came among them unheralded, without pomp or parade. He walked through the streets as if he were only a private citizen, and not the head of a mighty nation. He came not as a conqueror, not with bitterness in his heart, but with kindness. He came as a friend, to alleviate sorrow and suffering—to rebuild what had been destroyed."[26]

Colonel Thomas Thatcher Graves of Weitzel's staff had just left army headquarters in the Jefferson Davis house at the foot of Clay and Twelfth Streets when he saw the crowd coming, led by Lincoln, "walking with his usual long, careless stride, and looking about with an interested air and taking in everything." Hardly believing what he was seeing, Graves saluted the president, who asked, "Is it far to President Davis's house?"

Graves escorted him to the mansion, and there Lincoln seated himself in a chair in the reception room. Informed that it was Davis's study, he said, "This must have been President Davis's chair." Graves later wrote that Lincoln crossed his legs and looked far off with "a serious dreamy expression." The president then wanted to see the house. "We went pretty much over it," Graves remembered. "I retailed [*sic*] all that the housekeeper had told me, and he seemed interested in everything." As they descended the stairs into the study, General Weitzel, finally catching up, arrived "in breathless haste."[27]

This was not just a trip to satisfy Lincoln's curiosity. He also attended to business. John A. Campbell, the assistant Confederate secretary of war, a former U.S. Supreme court justice, and one of the three peace commissioners who had met with Lincoln and Seward on the *River Queen* in early February, called asking to see the president. Campbell was the highest-ranking Confederate official still in Richmond.

Lincoln met him and a handful of other Confederates, with General Weitzel sitting in as a witness, in the parlor of the Davis mansion, behind closed doors. Lincoln's primary obsession now that the war was virtually at an end was how the states in rebellion could be properly restored to their proper place in the Union. The meeting with Campbell was about how Virginia could be brought back.

After a short meeting, they agreed to meet again the next morning. Weitzel then took Lincoln and Porter in a carriage with a cavalry escort to the capitol, the burnt district, Libby Prison, and Castle Thunder, another bastille for captured Union soldiers. Lincoln passed the night on the *Malvern* anchored off Richmond.

The next morning, April 5, he met with Campbell a second time, on the ship, with General Weitzel again a witness. Lincoln handed Campbell a memorandum that reemphasized, as he had at the meeting with the Confederate peace commissioners in February, that he could not treat with any rebels until they had laid down their arms and surrendered, accepted nationwide emancipation, and bowed to the reestablishment of national authority. Campbell assured Lincoln that if he would allow the Virginia legislature to meet, it would at once repeal the ordinance of secession. This would amount to the virtual destruction of the Army of Northern Virginia, lead to the eventual surrender of all the rebel armies, and ensure peace in the shortest possible time. Lincoln said that he could not promise amnesty, but he had pardoning power and would go as far as he could to prevent further bloodshed.

After this second meeting, Lincoln told Weitzel that he would think the whole matter over carefully and probably send him instructions the next day. He then set off on the *Malvern* back to City Point.[28]

This Lincoln excursion to Richmond had been a junket that appalled many, upset by the president exposing himself in such a fashion in the very bosom of the Confederacy the day after its capital fell and was still in flames. But he did not seem to be bothered by any fear of personal danger to himself.

Lincoln greatly admired the writing genius of the popular humorist who went by the pen name Petroleum V. Nasby and once said he would swap the presidency if he could write the way Nasby did. For this occasion, Nasby summed it all up in his unique way: "Linkin rides into Richmond! A Illinois rale-splitter a buffoon, a ape, a goriller, a smutty joker, sets his self down in President Davis's cheer and rites dispatchis! . . . This ends the chapter. The Confederasy hez at last consentratid its last consentrate. It's ded. It's gathered up its feet, sed its last words, and deceest. . . . Farewell, vane world."[29]

C H A P T E R E L E V E N

THE ROAD TO APPOMATTOX

As Nasby was bidding farewell to the "vane world," Lincoln was wondering whether permitting the Virginia legislature to meet would be in vain. But after thinking about it overnight, he decided to give it a try. Back in City Point the next day, April 6, he sent General Weitzel a message.

"It has been intimated to me," he reminded Weitzel, "that the gentlemen who have acted as the Legislature of Virginia, in support of the rebellion, may now now [*sic*] desire to assemble at Richmond, and take measures to withdraw the Virginia troops, and other support from resistance to the General government. If they attempt it, give them permission and protection, until, if at all, they attempt some action hostile to the United States, in which case you will notify them and give them reasonable time to leave; & at the end of which time, arrest any who may remain."

At the same time he wired Grant, "I do not think it very probable that anything will come of this; but I have thought best to notify you, so that if you should see signs, you may understand them. From your recent dispatches it seems that you are pretty effectually withdrawing the Virginia troops from opposition to the Government. Nothing that I have done, or probably shall do, is to delay, hinder, or interfere with your work."[1]

Grant did indeed have all of Lee's army "effectually withdrawing"—on the run—with no thought of letup. There were signs of just how hurried Lee's withdrawal was. His path of retreat up the

Appomattox River was lined with stragglers and littered with arms, artillery, ammunition, burned or charred wagons, caissons, and ambulances. Striving to reach the road to Danville before being cut off, Lee was finding what Union major general Joshua Chamberlain was calling a "hard road to travel."

Virginia, Chamberlain believed, was "but a prison-pen; the Southside Railroad was the dead-line; the [Appomattox] River the Lethean stream," an underworld river of doom. Higher and higher up the road and river raced the two armies, "one with the frenzy of a forlorn hope; the other with the energy of fierce resolve." It had turned into a "week of flying fights," the Union force spearheaded by Sheridan's cavalry pressing with all speed to outflank Lee's "hurrying column."[2]

With Lincoln eagerly monitoring progress from City Point and kept informed by Grant, the pursuing army cut off nearly one-fourth of the retreating Confederate army on April 6 at what Chamberlain called "the ensanguined banks" of Little Sayler's Creek, the tributary of a larger, swampy Sayler's Creek meandering through Virginia farm country.[3] It was a battle fought in one day in three geographic parts simultaneously—and another disaster for Lee. Sheridan reported half a dozen Confederate generals, some seven thousand prisoners, fourteen pieces of artillery with caissons, and a large train of wagons captured.

Sheridan wired Grant, "If the thing is pressed I think Lee will surrender." Reading this, Lincoln wired Grant, "Let the *thing* be pressed."[4]

The remnants—which a young Confederate officer called "the flotsam and jetsam"[5]—of Lee's mortally crippled Army of Northern Virginia pressed on westward through a section of Virginia countryside as yet unscarred by war. The air was "sweet and pure, scented by opening buds and the breath of spring," as John Nicolay and John Hay, Lincoln's two personal secretaries, later described that countryside; "the early peach trees were in flower; the sylvan bypaths were slightly shaded by the pale-green foliage of leafing trees. Through these quiet solitudes the diminishing army of Lee plodded."[6] By now the way to Danville had been cut off. Lee changed the route of his retreat and headed for Lynchburg instead. Confederate troops were now calling their unrelenting pursuer "Sheridan, the Inevitable."[7]

A little before noon on April 7, Grant rode into the little village of Farmville on the south bank of the Appomattox River. There he set up headquarters on the broad piazza of the village hotel and opened a correspondence with Lee on the subject of surrender—to stop "any further effusion of blood." Lee answered that evening, reciprocating Grant's desire to avoid useless effusion of blood and asking for terms.

The next morning Grant replied, "There is but one condition I would insist upon, namely: that the men and officers surrendered shall be disqualified for taking up arms again against the Government of the United States until properly exchanged." He offered to meet Lee anywhere agreeable to him for "arranging definitely" the terms of surrender.

It was apparent to Grant that Lee's army was "rapidly crumbling." However, that evening, about midnight, Lee answered that he did not intend to surrender his army and would not meet Grant for that purpose. But to discuss "the restoration of peace," he proposed a meeting at ten o'clock the next morning, Sunday April 9, on the old stage road to Richmond between the picket lines of the two armies.

Grant, who had been suffering through these exchanges with a sick headache, replied that because he had "no authority to treat on the subject of peace," the meeting Lee proposed for that morning "could lead to no good." But he assured Lee that he was as anxious for peace as Lee was and said that "by the South laying down their arms they will hasten that most desirable event, save thousands of human lives, and hundreds of millions of property not yet destroyed."

As these notes were being exchanged, the screws were being ever tightened on Lee's army. Though still suffering with his headache, Grant spurned an ambulance. He mounted his horse, Cincinnati, and rode on toward New Store, some ten miles from a little hamlet called Appomattox Court House. He was traveling with General George Gordon Meade's Army of the Potomac close on the Confederate rear. Sheridan had by this time at last placed himself on Lee's line of retreat at Appomattox Court House, buttressed by overwhelming infantry support. With nowhere now to go, the Confederate retreat abruptly stopped.

Lee halted a short distance in the rear of the Confederate line at three o'clock in the morning on April 9. Still believing there might be hope, he called for Colonel C. S. Venable of his staff and sent him to Major General John Gordon, commanding the Confederate vanguard, to ask him if he could break through. Venable later wrote, "I found General Gordon and General Fitz Lee on their front line in the dim light of the morning arranging an attack." To the question Lee asked, Gordon replied, "Tell General Lee I have fought my corps to a frazzle, and I fear I can do nothing unless I am heavily supported by [James] Longstreet's corps."

Told this, the impossible, Lee said, "Then there is nothing left me but to go and see General Grant, and I would rather die a thousand deaths."[8]

Grant was overtaken on the wagon road with a final message from Lee: he was now willing to meet on Grant's terms—the surrender of the Army of Northern Virginia. At the same time, Grant received a note from Meade that at Lee's request, he had granted a short truce to see how this all played out.

At eleven thirty in the morning Grant dismounted, sat on a grassy bank, and wrote Lee that he was about four miles west of Walker's Church and would push forward to the front to meet him, expecting as he rode to receive notice from Lee saying where he wished to meet. Grant then remounted and rode on at a trot for Appomattox Court House, telling Horace Porter of his staff, "The pain in my head seemed to leave me the moment I got Lee's letter."[9]

It was Palm Sunday and the war had come down to this—to the little village of Appomattox Court House, with its half dozen houses, in rural Virginia eighty-five miles west of Richmond. Grant rode into the town, named for the Appomattoc Indians, in the early afternoon. He turned onto its single street and stopped in front of a two-story brick house standing a short distance back from the road. Lee's gray horse, Traveler, and Confederate colonel Charles Marshall's mare grazed in the front yard in the charge of an orderly in gray. Grant climbed the seven steps to the house's ample front porch and entered its sitting room about one thirty.

This was Wilmer McLean's house, and this was the irony of ironies. Its owner, with stunning justification, might have been thinking,

"Why me, Lord?" On July 21, 1861, the day of the first big battle of the war across Bull Run Creek at Manassas, Virginia, McLean had owned and lived in a farmhouse on that battlefield. The house had been commandeered in the heat of the battle for the headquarters of Confederate general P. G. T. Beauregard. After the battle, to get as far away from the war as possible and still live in Virginia, McLean had moved to this remote little village on the Appomattox River, where it was inconceivable that the war would ever reach, and purchased this two-story brick house. A house he owned and lived in had been at the center of the first great scene of the war. Now, four years later and many miles away, another house he owned and lived in was about to become the stage for its very last. War and destiny dogged Wilmer McLean. He had not escaped either one.[10]

Lee was awaiting Grant in the sitting room, seated beside a small, oval table near the front window in the corner opposite the door. Colonel Marshall, Lee's military secretary, stood at his left. Grant entered, the two generals greeted one another, and Grant took a seat at a marble-topped table in the center of the room. A small group of Grant's generals quietly filed in along the walls, "very much," Horace Porter later wrote, "as people enter a sick-chamber when they expect to find the patient dangerously ill." Most remained standing, although some sat on the sofa and the few chairs in the room.[11]

Grant and Lee sat within ten feet, facing one another. The distance between the two men could also be measured by years, dress, physical dimensions, and appearance. Lee was sixteen years older than his counterpart. He was an erect six feet tall. His hair and full beard had turned silver-gray in the war. He was dressed for the occasion in a travel-stained but clean dress uniform of Confederate gray buttoned to the throat. He wore top boots handsomely spurred. A long military sword with a jewel-studded hilt hung at his side. A pair of long, gray buckskin gauntlets lay beside him on the table.

Grant, just in from riding the road to Appomattox, was five feet, nine inches tall, a slightly stooped three inches shorter than Lee. His hair and beard were nut brown, without a single strand of gray. His single-breasted blouse of dark-blue flannel was unbuttoned at the front, revealing a waistcoat beneath. His top boots were ordinary, and his trousers, tucked inside, were mud-spattered. He wore no spurs, no sword hung at his side, and only the shoulder straps with their three stars told the world he was a lieutenant general. He looked otherwise like any soldier in the ranks.

Grant's feelings, at this moment of finally meeting with his adversary, had switched from being "quite jubilant" when he earlier received Lee's agreement to surrender to "sad and depressed," not ready now for "rejoicing at the downfall" of so valiant a foe.[12] The two generals talked for a time of days in the Old Army. Both had served in the Mexican-American War, Lee as an engineer on General Winfield Scott's staff, Grant as a regimental quartermaster. Finally Lee reminded Grant of "the object of our meeting."[13] Grant motioned for a pen and began to write out the conditions of the surrender: All Confederate officers and soldiers were to be paroled and allowed to return to their homes, not to be disturbed by U.S. authority as long as they observed their paroles and the laws where they lived. Officers would be allowed to keep their sidearms, horses, and private baggage.

Lee saw these as gratifying terms. But what of the Confederate cavalrymen and artillerists, who, unlike Union soldiers, owned the horses they rode and would be returning to wasted fields at home? They would need the horses they were riding. Reconsidering, Grant agreed that common soldiers could also keep their horses. No sword of surrender was asked for, none taken.

These were liberal, humane terms, and the compassionate handprints of Abraham Lincoln were all over them. They were, indeed, pure Lincoln. Compassionate reconciliation was what the president wanted, and Grant understood that. In a meeting Lincoln had held on March 27–28 on the *River Queen* with Grant, Admiral Porter, and General Sherman, who had come over for it from his army in North Carolina, the president had instructed, "Let them all go, officers and all. I want submission, and no more bloodshed. Let them have their horses to plow with, and, if you like, their guns to shoot crows with. I want no one punished; treat them liberally all round. We want these people to return to their allegiance to the Union and submit to the laws. Again I say, give them the most liberal and honorable terms."[14]

Lee riding from the McLean house after surrendering his Army of Northern Virginia at Appomattox. He had said he would rather "die a thousand deaths" than go surrender to Grant. Courtesy of the Library of Congress, LC-USZ62–11095.

A little before four o'clock in the afternoon, the meeting between Grant and Lee ended, and the two generals shook hands. Lee bowed to the other Union officers present and left the house. Grant followed, and as Lee mounted and prepared to leave the yard, Grant stepped down from the porch and, moving toward the Confederate general, raised his hat in salute, an act of courtesy and respect repeated by all the Union officers present.

When news of the surrender reached the troops, many Confederate soldiers wept. Some of the Union soldiers began firing salutes in celebration. Hearing this, Grant ordered them stopped immediately. "The war is over," he said; "the rebels are our countrymen again; and the best sign of rejoicing after the victory will be to abstain from all demonstrations in the field."[15] This act, too, smacked of Abraham Lincoln.

Reminded as he rode away from the McLean house for his headquarters camp that he had not yet informed the government, Grant dismounted by the roadside, sat on a large rock, and wrote this brief wire to Stanton at four thirty in the afternoon on April 9: "General Lee surrendered the Army of Northern Virginia this afternoon on terms proposed by myself. The accompanying additional correspondence will show the conditions fully."[16]

The trappings of surrender followed this "crowning act of the war."[17] "The charges," Horace Porter wrote, "were now withdrawn from the guns, the camp-fires were left to smolder in their ashes, the horses were detached from the cannon to be hitched to the plow, and the Army of the Union and the Army of Northern Virginia turned their backs upon each other for the first time in four long, bloody years."[18]

Tears fell throughout the South. The grieving Confederate soldiers about to start home cried for themselves, their beloved general, and their lost cause. A young Georgia woman wrote, "It is all over with us now. . . . No more talk about fighting to the last ditch; the last ditch has already been reached."[19]

Those, however, were not the sentiments of her president, Jefferson Davis. For him the last ditch had not been reached. Although he was exhausted and feeble in body, he was still resolute in mind. On the night of April 2 Davis and his party—several members of his cabinet and other government officials, some members of the Virginia legislature, and a few private citizens of distinction—left Richmond after eleven o'clock, pressing on midnight. They reached Danville, on the south bank of the Dan River within three miles of the North Carolina border, the next day at about three o'clock in the afternoon. There they waited until the night of April 10, the day after Lee surrendered, then started south into North Carolina, headed for Georgia.[20]

The Confederate postmaster general John H. Reagan, who was traveling with Davis, knew that the president "would not leave Confederate soil while there was a Confederate regiment on it." Davis intended to avoid capture, organize a joint force, and carry on the war.[21]

Lincoln, of course, wished he wouldn't. Indeed, Lincoln wished Davis would just go away, leave the country. He would not stop him. When General Weitzel had taken Lincoln to Libby Prison and Castle Thunder during his visit to Richmond on April 4, he had asked the president how he should treat the conquered people. Lincoln had said, "If I were in your place I'd let 'em up easy, let 'em up easy."[22]

He had been making the suggestion to "let 'em up easy" to others besides Weitzel. He told Speaker of the House Schuyler Colfax, "Scare them out of the country," and "if they leave, no attempt will be made to hinder them. Then we can be magnanimous to all the rest and have peace and quiet in the whole land." To Assistant Secretary of War Charles A. Dana, he said, "When you have got an elephant by the hind leg, and he's trying to run away, it's best to let him run." He later told his cabinet, "I should not be sorry to have them out of the country, but I should be for following them up pretty close to make sure of their going."[23]

Soldiers in the war had called battle "seeing the elephant." This different kind of elephant, the one bent on running, Lincoln was more than pleased to let run.

CHAPTER TWELVE

WAR'S END

By April 8 Lincoln was also certain of his own going. He had been at City Point for sixteen days, living the drama of war with Grant's army. It was the longest he had been away from Washington in the four years of his presidency. Now it was time to return.

Lincoln was concerned about his secretary of state, William Seward. On the evening of April 5, Stanton had wired Lincoln that Seward had been "thrown from his carriage." Seward's "shoulder bone at the head of the joint [was] broken off" and "his head and face [were] much bruised," he told Lincoln. "He is in my opinion dangerously injured. I think your presence here is needed." Lincoln wired Grant, "This, with other matters, will take me to Washington soon."[1]

"Soon" was to be the night of April 8. That day, before leaving, Lincoln spent five hours touring hospitals, consoling and shaking the hands of the wounded, both Union and Confederate. At eleven that evening the *River Queen* left City Point. All the next day, as Grant was taking Lee's surrender in the McLean house at Appomattox Court House, Lincoln was en route, arriving at the capital about sundown. He went immediately to see the bedridden Seward, whose jaw and right arm near the shoulder joint were broken from his fall. There Lincoln lay full length next to him. Resting on his elbows, his face near his secretary of state's, he told Seward, "I think we are near the end at last." He recounted Grant's victories and told Seward of his visit to Richmond.[2]

All of Washington was lit with bonfires. The city, still aglow from the fall of Richmond, was now intense with anticipation of the ultimate good news from Virginia—surrender and war's end. "We live on tiptoe for events," one Washingtonian wrote.[3] That evening the news finally came—telegraphed from Grant to Lincoln—that the Army of Northern Virginia had surrendered.

A five-hundred-gun salute at daylight the next morning, April 10, shook the city and rattled windows on Lafayette Square—"Secretary Stanton's way of telling the people that the Army of Northern Virginia had at last laid down it arms, and that peace had come again," Noah Brooks explained.[4]

Cities everywhere in the North erupted in joy. Bells tolled, guns fired, cannons roared, bonfires raged, steam engines whistled, fireworks exploded, speeches were delivered. Throughout the day, despite rain and mud, Washington serenaded Lincoln. An impromptu procession started from the Navy Yard and headed for the White House, dragging six boat howitzers and picking up "hurrahing legions" along the way.[5] As the throng turned up Fifteenth Street, it had swelled to a concourse of more than three thousand cheering participants. Bands played and the howitzers roared as the marchers crowded onto the White House portico, the carriageway, and the pavements on either side. Call after call went out to the president, and at length the crowd flushed him out. He appeared at a White House window to three "loud and hearty cheers."

After a few words, Lincoln said, "I have always thought 'Dixie' one of the best tunes I have ever heard. Our adversaries over the way attempted to appropriate it, but I insisted yesterday that we fairly captured it. I presented the question to the Attorney General, and he gave it as his legal opinion that it is our lawful prize." Lincoln requested that the song be played now, and the band struck it up and followed with "Yankee Doodle" as Lincoln listened from the window.

"Now," he said, "give three good hearty cheers for General Grant and all under his command," then "three more cheers for our gallant Navy." That done, Lincoln disappeared from the window to parting cheers from the crowd.[6]

But the serenading was not over. Another immense crowd with a band collected before the White House that evening. Lincoln would not make a speech, however, instead promising more the next evening. "I would then be much better prepared to say what I have to say than I am now or can be this evening," he told the throng. Then, he promised, "I will endeavor to say something, and not make a mistake, without at least trying carefully to avoid it."[7]

The next evening, April 11, although under misty skies, Washington was again ablaze with lights, "in its brightest garb of joy . . . all pervaded with a generous exaltation." An enormous crowd once more collected around the White House for another "jollification," expecting a few words from Lincoln celebrating victory and exulting in the happy outcome of the war.

That is not what they got from their president.

Responses to serenades were generally extemporaneous. What Lincoln intended to say was so important to him that he had written this one out. "It is true," he told Noah Brooks, "that I don't usually read a speech, but I am going to say something to-night that may be important. I am going to talk about reconstruction, and sometimes I am betrayed into saying things that other people don't like." As Brooks held a light, Lincoln began reading his written speech, dropping the pages to the floor one by one as he finished them. As they dropped, Tad scrambled about under his feet snatching them up and imploring him for another.[8]

Lincoln's priorities had emphatically shifted. For four years winning the war had been front and center. That was done. Now his mind was totally consumed with recalling, as soon as possible, the Southern states back into the Union—"the re-inauguration of the national authority"—under a "policy of pardon and forgiveness."[9] Lincoln's intent was to make these enemies friends again.

However, though now front and center, reconstruction of a beaten South was hardly a new thought in Lincoln's mind. He had been edging the country toward it for more than a year. He had been appointing military governors in insurrectionary states. He had issued an amnesty and reconstruction proclamation in December 1863. Under that proclamation, he had been pushing liberal plans for the reconstruction of loyal state governments in Arkansas, Louisiana, and Tennessee.

None of this was going to be easy, and it would have to be done against the angry opposition of a cadre of fierce Radical Republicans in Congress. He had enraged the Radicals in July 1864 when he vetoed their reconstruction bill. Congress wanted to control this process, and the congressmen most interested in controlling it were the sort "thirsting for a general hanging."[10] Secretary of the Navy Gideon Welles had called this group "a wild, radical element" that wished to treat the South no longer as states, but as territories without rights that must have a new birth or creation by permission of a vengeful Congress.[11]

That, in Lincoln's mind, would not do. As the Marquis de Chambrun suggested, he was going to "stand for clemency against all opposition."[12] This did not mean that Lincoln would not work with the Radicals in his party to try to find a common ground. Lincoln could not bring himself to dislike them, despite their opposition to him and their antipathy to his reconstruction program. Musing one day with John Hay, he said, "They are utterly lawless—the unhandiest devils in the world to deal with—but after all their faces are set Zionwards."[13]

In his speech responding to the serenade on the night of April 11, Lincoln was taking his stand immediately. He told Noah Brooks that he "wanted to give his views on reconstruction as early and as frequently as possible."[14] His view of reconstruction was not what the serenaders had come to hear, but it was what he wanted them to hear.

He eased into it, calling first for a national thanksgiving. "We meet this evening, not in sorrow," he said, "but in gladness of heart. The evacuation of Petersburg and Richmond, and the surrender of the principal insurgent army, give hope of a righteous and speedy peace whose joyous expression can not be restrained. In the midst of this, however, He from Whom all blessings flow, must not be forgotten."

Then he got down to what was really on his mind: reconstruction. It is "fraught with great difficulty," he told the serenaders. "Unlike the case of a war between independent nations, there is no authorized organ for us to treat with. No one man has authority to give up the rebellion for any other man. We simply must begin with, and mould from, disorganized and discordant elements. Nor is it a small additional embarrassment that we, the loyal people, differ among ourselves as to the mode, manner, and means of reconstruction."

Lincoln did not believe his was the only acceptable plan. He was open to others within the parameters of his cherished clemency. "We all agree," he said, "that the seceded States, so called, are out of their proper practical relation with the Union; and that the sole object of the government, civil and military, in regard to those States is to again get them into that proper practical relation."

He saw Louisiana, a state on which he had been concentrating, as very ready and nearly back into that practical relationship. "Some twelve thousand voters in the heretofore slave-state of Louisiana," he said, "have sworn allegiance to the Union, assumed to be the rightful political power of the State, held elections, organized a State government, adopted a free-state constitution, giving the benefit of public schools equally to black and white, and empowering the Legislature to confer the elective franchise upon the colored man. Their Legislature has already voted to ratify the constitutional amendment recently passed by Congress, abolishing slavery throughout the nation. These twelve thousand persons are thus fully committed to the Union, and to perpetual freedom in the state—committed to the very things, and nearly all the things the nation wants—and they ask the nations [*sic*] recognition, and its assistance to make good their committal."

"Now, if we reject, and spurn them," Lincoln warned, "we do our utmost to disorganize and disperse them. We in effect say to the white men 'You are worthless, or worse—we will neither help you, nor be helped by you.' To the blacks we say 'This cup of liberty which these, your old masters, hold to your lips, we will dash from you, and leave you to the chances of gathering the spilled and scattered contents in some vague and undefined when, where, and how.'" He continued, "If this course, discouraging and paralyzing both white and black, has any tendency to bring Louisiana into proper practical relations with the Union, I have, so far, been unable to perceive it. If, on the contrary, we recognize, and sustain the new government of Louisiana the converse of all this is made true."

What he has said about Louisiana, Lincoln said, "will apply generally to other States," at the same time recognizing that each has its own peculiarities. At least one thing Lincoln said would have put him in closer tune with the Radicals, who wanted the right to vote extended to black men: "It is also unsatisfactory to some that the elective franchise is not given to the colored man. I would myself prefer that it were now conferred on the very intelligent, and those who serve our cause as soldiers." That was not going as far as the Radicals wished, but it was a step in their direction.

That was what Lincoln said to the serenaders, and many were disappointed, as they wished to hear bright notes of triumphant victory. Instead, these were dull notes played in a minor key. Moreover, Lincoln promised that it would not be the last they would hear about this subject from him. "In the present '*situation*' as the phrase goes," he advised them, "it may be my duty to make some new announcement to the people of the South. I am considering, and shall not fail to act, when satisfied that action will be proper."[15]

Lincoln said of the speech, "I am trying to blaze a way through the swamp."[16] The Radical Massachusetts senator Charles Sumner, hungering for racial equality and for congressional command over reconstruction, said, "So far as I can see, his speech has fallen very dead."[17] The Lincoln-hating Democratic *New York World* wrote, "Mr. Lincoln gropes, in his speech, like a traveler in an unknown country without a map."[18]

The *Daily National Intelligencer* in Washington, however, called it a "remarkable speech, wise in *sentiment* . . . pervaded by the logic of the heart" with a "keeness and clearness of perception and grasp of thought . . . certainly remarkable." It is a speech, the *Intelligencer* said, of "practical statesmanship," with an "eminent sense of justice." It is "from a lofty stand-point; it soars away above party." Lincoln's aim, as the *Intelligencer* saw it, "appears to be to find and do the right, within the limits of the Constitution and the laws." With "this great and good speech . . . he has opened wide the gate to restoration; and thus far, he has grandly performed his part."[19]

One listener in the crowd detested the speech for a deadly reason. John Wilkes Booth, a prominent actor from a prominent thespian family and an ardent Southern sympathizer, racist, and Lincoln hater, bristled. He believed the president was conceding too much to the Radicals. Hearing his words favoring a limited franchise for black men, he muttered, "This means nigger citizenship." He vowed, "Now, by God, I'll put him through. That is the last speech he will ever make."[20]

The next morning, April 12, reconstruction was still on Lincoln's mind. But Virginia was disappointing him. His experiment—allowing members of its legislature to reconvene to withdraw the state from the rebellion—was not working out. John Campbell, with whom he had struck a deal, had misconstrued his intent.

"I have just seen Judge Campbell's letter to you of the 7th," he wired General Weitzel in Richmond. "He assumes as appears to me that I have called the insurgent Legislature of Virginia together, as the rightful Legislature of the State, to settle all differences with the United States. I have done no such thing."

Lincoln told Weitzel, "I spoke of them not as a Legislature, but as 'the gentlemen who have *acted* as the Legislature of Virginia in support of the rebellion.' I did this on purpose to exclude the assumption that I was recognizing them as a *rightful* body. I dealt with them as men having power *de facto* to do a specific thing, towit, 'to withdraw the Virginia troops, and other support from resistance to the General Government.'" He had meant this and nothing more.

"Let my letter to you, and the paper to Judge Campbell both be withdrawn or, countermanded, and he be notified of it," Lincoln ordered Weitzel. "Do not now allow them to assemble; but if any have come, allow them safe-return to their homes."[21]

While Lincoln was dealing with reconstruction of the Southern states, Secretary of War Stanton was dealing with deconstruction of the Union armies. On April 13, "after mature consideration and consultation" with Grant, he issued a general order halting the draft and curtailing all recruiting and purchasing of arms and ammunition for war. He ordered the number of general and staff officers in the army drastically cut back. The plan now was to fix the soldier-to-population ratio at 1 to 1,000, in line with the ratio of 1 to 963 before the war. Finally, Stanton's order, to be carried out immediately, removed all military restrictions on trade and commerce with the

South, consistent with public safety. People could now go to and return from the South at will, as before the war.[22]

All this was yet another arrow in Lincoln's quiver of clemency. In what seemed a wholly contradictory policy, Lincoln had tried from the beginning to exercise the utmost possible compassion while waging what became the bloodiest war in American history. He had said after his reelection, "So long as I have been here I have not willingly planted a thorn in any man's bosom."[23]

He had also said from the start, "I suppose I will have to run the machine as I find it." That is what he had tried to do for four long years. He told his Illinois friend John M. Palmer that he had never had a policy—his hope had been to save the Union, and his policy simply had been to try "to do what seemed best each day, as each day came."[24] When the visiting Prince de Joinville of France asked him what was his policy, Lincoln had replied, "I have none. I pass my life in preventing the storm from blowing down the tent, and I drive in the pegs as fast as they are pulled up."[25]

Lincoln's two young private secretaries, John Nicolay and John Hay, had found Lincoln "extremely unmethodical." "It was a four-years struggle on Nicolay's part and mine," Hay wrote, "to get him to adopt some systematic rules." The president, Hay believed, had simply "pursued those labors which will carry his name to distant ages. There was little order or system about it."[26]

But it had worked. "His eyes—surely the saddest and most solemn that ever looked on the wars of a sorrowing world," a friend wrote, "had seen the surrender of Lee, his feet had pressed the recovered soil of Virginia, had trodden the streets of the enemies' capital, and he now saw himself ruler of the whole recovered country, with no slaves upon its soil and with no armed foe within its borders."[27] It seemed to William O. Stoddard, a third personal secretary for a time, that the Civil War was "the terrible furnace time, during which . . . the old nation melted away and a new nation was moulded."[28]

April 14 was a beautiful sunny day that gave way to a patchy fog. The man who had "melted away" the old and "moulded" the new was planning to attend a play that evening at Ford's Theater on Tenth Street, called *Our American Cousin*—a light diversion at the end of a heavy four years.

Beginning the day, he had breakfast with his son Robert, who had arrived from the scene of Lee's surrender. During the morning, Lincoln conferred at length with Congressman Schuyler Colfax of Indiana, who was preparing a visit to the West Coast. Later in the morning, he interviewed Senator John P. Hale of New Hampshire, the newly appointed minister to Spain. Also that the morning, he received many members of Congress who had come to congratulate him on the successful end of the war, and he went for a short drive with General Grant, who was in town for a cabinet meeting.

At the meeting, from eleven in the morning to two in the afternoon, Grant reported on the surrender of Confederate forces at Appomattox. Secretary of War Stanton presented a draft of a plan for reestablishing authority in the Confederate states. And there was a discussion of what was to be done with President Davis and other Confederate leaders.

After the meeting, Lincoln lunched with Mrs. Lincoln in the private parlor of the White House and later interviewed Vice President Johnson. In the late afternoon, the president and Mrs. Lincoln went for a drive together, where Lincoln talked of the time when they could return to Illinois and live quietly.

At eight thirty in the evening, the couple left for the theater. Lincoln and his wife would not see the time when they could return to Illinois and live the rest of their lives quietly. John Wilkes Booth, with a small pistol and a shot through the president's head, had fulfilled his vow that Lincoln's speech on reconstruction would be his last.[29] Lincoln died early the next morning in a house across the street from the theater.

John Hay, who had shared those four years in the White House with Lincoln and also possessed a gift for putting words together, summed what he believed about this president:

> He bore the sorrows of the nation in his own heart; he suffered deeply, not only from disappointments, from treachery, from hope deferred, from the open assaults of enemies and from

the sincere anger of discontented friends, but also from the world wide distress and affliction which flowed from the great conflict in which he was engaged and which he could not evade. One of the most tender and compassionate of men, he was forced to give orders which cost thousands of lives; by nature a man of order and thrift, he saw the daily spectacle of unutterable waste and destruction which he could not prevent. The cry of the widow and the orphan was always in his ears; the awful responsibility resting upon him as the protector of an imperilled republic kept him true to his duty, but could not make him unmindful of the intimate details of that vast sum of human misery involved in civil war.[30]

EPILOGUE
THE GRAND FAREWELL

Lincoln, murdered by the assassin as he watched the play, did not live to see the Thirteenth Amendment finally ratified or the South reconstructed with the compassion he wished. He did not live to see the Confederate armies in the other theaters of the war surrender, dominoes falling after Appomattox. He did not live to see Johnston agreeing to surrender terms with Sherman in North Carolina on April 18—and then again on April 26, when Stanton, reacting harshly in the chaotic wake of the assassination, thought Sherman's initial terms too lenient. (Would Lincoln have thought so?)

He did not live to see Confederate forces in Alabama, Mississippi, and East Louisiana surrender on May 4; in Florida and South Georgia on May 10; in North Georgia on May 12; in the Trans-Mississippi West on May 26; and the Confederate Indians in Indian Territory on June 23.

He did not live to see the last faint candle of the Confederacy gutter and go out on May 10, when Jefferson Davis was captured outside Irwinville, Georgia—the elephant who had not succeeded in running away.

And he did not live to see his victorious armies march one more time—on May 23 and 24, 1865, down Pennsylvania Avenue. Following the key final surrenders, the armies began moving toward Washington for a "grand farewell."[1] The two great armies of the East and West—more than two hundred thousand battle-tried men—would be assembled in one body in one place for the first and only time, "gathered together from every battle-field of the war."[2] Trains began arriving several days before, bringing in thousands for the spectacle.

The eastern army marched first on May 23, with 108 regiments of infantry, twenty-nine of cavalry, and thirty-three battalions of artillery. It was "a great day, a day of days" in the capital, Noah Brooks exulted. The weather was perfect. Two or three days of rain had "cooled the air and laid the dust." The armies of the East marched down Pennsylvania Avenue, bayonets glistening, sabers flashing, banners snapping, music crashing. Schools had closed, and children were massed in the porticoes and terraces on the northern end of the Capitol, waving miniature flags and greeting the marching soldiers with bursts of patriotic song. The new president, Andrew Johnson, and other dignitaries watched the armies pass from a reviewing stand on Pennsylvania Avenue nearest the White House. For five and a half hours the blue lines of the army of the East passed, sixty soldiers abreast, their bayonets fixed and gleaming in the sun.[3]

Grand Review of the Armies in Washington, DC, May 23–24, 1865, marching "back into the heart of the people from whence [they] came." Courtesy of the National Archives, drawing no. 111-BA-69.

On the second day, May 24, the armies of the West marched for their five and a half hours, 180 regiments of infantry with their artillery and cavalry components, foragers and all. Down the avenue, marveled Union general Joshua Chamberlain, poured a "shining river of steel" from the West, a "mighty march" of "far-marched men"—"that flaming bolt which cut the Confederacy in two."[4]

As the head of Sherman's infantry reached the Treasury building, an improvised chorus in the stands began singing "John Brown's Body," the soldiers' anthem that this same army had sung while leaving Atlanta in flames and entering a Columbia soon to be in flames. The chorus "was at once taken up by the advancing column," an officer wrote, "regiment after regiment, until it became a great wave of sound rising and falling in rhythmic cadence. The long vista glittered as a river of fire, with sunlight reflected from the thousands of bayonets undulating with the easy swinging stride of the western troops. The sight and the refrain combined came upon eye and ear in bewildering, and I confess, to me, overpowering emotion."[5]

The two armies passed, Chamberlain wrote, "like the children of Israel walled by the friendly Red Sea. Around us and above, murmurs, lightnings and thunders of greeting. . . . All the way up the avenue a tumult of sound and motion."[6]

When the two armies—a vast concourse of citizen soldiers "trained on a hundred battlefields"—had passed, "no one doubted any more that this was the greatest army that ever went to war," an army of men melting "back into the heart of the people from whence it came," heroes all, claimed by the whole country "as a part of themselves."[7] It was an unprecedented spectacle, one that would never be repeated, but one that would always be remembered.

And so, the poet Walt Whitman wrote, "good-bye to the war." The real one, he predicted, "will never get in the books."[8]

Abraham Lincoln, who had led the country through the real war and had known this war perhaps more intimately than any other man or woman, was an unprecedented man, not likely to be a man repeated, but one who also would always be vividly remembered.

IN APPRECIATION

NOTES

SOURCES CITED

INDEX

IN APPRECIATION

In writing any kind of book, the author often experiences a mix of loneliness and cries for help, ending in relief and exaltation. This one was no different. To do the research for a book of history requires a lot of reaching out to libraries, both my own and others. As with all the books I have written since moving to Texas, I have drawn heavily on the three great university libraries in the Dallas–Fort Worth metroplex: Texas Christian, Southern Methodist, and the University of Texas at Arlington.

I am indebted to four readers from Southern Illinois University Press who contributed excellent suggestions, beginning with my editor, Sylvia Frank Rodrigue, followed by Sara Vaughn Gabbard and Richard W. Etulain. The fourth, an anonymous outside reader who read the manuscript in close detail, made marvelous contributions.

Two who guided the book through the editing process—Wayne Larsen, the project editor at Southern Illinois University Press, and Joyce Bond, a freelance editor—deserve multiple thanks. Their contributions, in particular Ms. Bond's careful, thoughtful, detailed, and intelligent editing, have made this a better, more accurate book.

I also owe a special debt to my friend Everett Chasen, who volunteered his time and did valuable research for the book at the Library of Congress and elsewhere in Washington, DC. For the excellent map to help guide you through Lincoln's presence at the seat of the war in its dying days, I am grateful to George Skoch.

And nothing would be possible without the loving support always of my wife, Kathleen Dianne Lively.

To all, many thanks.

NOTES

Prologue: Worth More Than a Battle Won

1. French, *Witness to the Young Republic*, 460.
2. Strong, *Diary*, 511.
3. *New York Herald*, November 17, 1864.
4. Ford, *Cycle of Adams Letters*, 2:223, 229.
5. Grant, *Papers*, 12:398; Mitgang, *Abraham Lincoln*, 440.
6. *Washington Star*, November 11, 1864. See also Browne, *Every-Day Life of Abraham Lincoln*, 548–49.
7. Lincoln, "Response to a Serenade," November 8, 1864, *Collected Works*, 8:96.
8. Brooks, *Lincoln Observed*, 145.
9. Lincoln, "Response to a Serenade," November 10, 1864, *Collected Works*, 8:101.

1. Armies on the March

1. Wainwright, *Diary of Battle*, 480–81.
2. Hay, *Inside Lincoln's White House*, 251, 263.
3. U.S. War Department, *War of the Rebellion*, ser. 1, vol. 39, part 3, 162 (hereafter cited as O.R.).
4. Porter, *Campaigning with Grant*, 293.
5. O.R., ser. 1, vol. 39, part 3, 162.
6. This Grant-Sherman exchange is in Sherman, *Memoirs*, 2:639–42.
7. Johnson and Buel, *Battles and Leaders*, 4:426–27.
8. Sherman, *Memoirs*, 2:651–52.
9. Angle and Miers, *Tragic Years*, 2:924.
10. Johnson and Buel, *Battles and Leaders*, 4:663.
11. Sherman, *Memoirs*, 2:655.
12. Nichols, *Story of the Great March*, 38.
13. Connolly, *Three Years in the Army of the Cumberland*, 301–2.
14. McWhirter, *Battle Hymns*, 44.
15. Jenkins, "Origin of the Famous War Song of John Brown," 210.
16. Sherman, *Memoirs*, 2:656.
17. Angle and Miers, *Tragic Years*, 2:937.
18. Nichols, *Story of the Great March*, 72.
19. Nevins, *War for the Union*, 4:174.
20. O.R., ser. 1, vol. 45, part 1, 1170.
21. Hood, *Advance and Retreat*, 292, 296.
22. Johnson and Buel, *Battles and Leaders*, 4:446–48.

23. Cleland, "Second March to the Ohio," 226.
24. Angle and Miers, *Tragic Years*, 2:941.
25. Sexton, "Captain of Infantry at the Battle of Franklin," 473.
26. Speed, "Battle of Franklin," 72.
27. Johnson and Buel, *Battles and Leaders*, 4:451.
28. Sexton, "Captain of Infantry at the Battle of Franklin," 474.
29. Schofield, *Forty-Six Years in the Army*, 177–78.
30. Johnson and Buel, *Battles and Leaders*, 4:451, 453.
31. Speed, "Battle of Franklin," 94.
32. Johnson, *Campfire and Battlefield*, 429.
33. Cleland, "Second March to the Ohio," 229.
34. Sexton, "Captain of Infantry at the Battle of Franklin," 477, 483.
35. Hutchins, "Battle of Franklin, Tennessee," 281.
36. Watkins, *"Co. Aytch,"* 218.
37. Alexander, *Fighting for the Confederacy*, 498.
38. Speed, "Battle of Franklin," 97.
39. Angle and Miers, *Tragic Years*, 2:942.
40. Johnson and Buel, *Battles and Leaders*, 4:435.
41. Milchrist, "Reflections of a Subaltern," 464–65.
42. Watkins, *"Co. Aytch,"* 216.

2. Unfinished Business

1. Nicolay, *With Lincoln in the White House*, 168.
2. Lincoln, "Response to a Serenade," December 6, 1864, *Collected Works*, 8:154.
3. Fehrenbacher and Fehrenbacher, *Recollected Words*, 403; Lincoln, "Response to a Serenade," December 6, 1864, *Collected Works*, 8:154.
4. Brooks, "Personal Recollections of Abraham Lincoln," 227.
5. Angle and Miers, *Living Lincoln*, 634.
6. Strong, *Diary*, 518.
7. Davis, *Papers*, 61.
8. Porter, *Campaigning with Grant*, 313.
9. Coffin, *Four Years of Fighting*, 393.
10. Andrews, *War-Time Journal of a Georgia Girl*, 63–64, 47.
11. Johnson and Buel, *Battles and Leaders*, 4:667.
12. Belknap, "Recollections of a Bummer," 15.
13. Johnson and Buel, *Battles and Leaders*, 4:674.
14. Johnson, *Campfire and Battlefield*, 427.
15. Rhodes, *History of the United States*, 5:28.
16. Kerr, "From Atlanta to Raleigh," 213.
17. Sherman, *Memoirs*, 2:664.
18. Brooks, *Mr. Lincoln's Washington*, 390–91.
19. Welles, *Diary*, 2:179.

20. Brooks, *Lincoln Observed*, 151.
21. Lincoln, "To Samuel A. Cony and Others," November 15, 1864, "To William M. Stone and Others," November 29, 1864, and "Annual Message to Congress," December 6, 1864, *Collected Works*, 8:108, 124, 149, 150, 151.
22. Lincoln, "Annual Message to Congress," December 6, 1864, *Collected Works*, 8:136–53.
23. Brooks, *Lincoln Observed*, 155.
24. Bates, "Diary," 427.
25. Lincoln, "To James Speed," December 1, 1864, *Collected Works*, 8:126, 126–27n.
26. Goodwin, *Team of Rivals*, 676.
27. I am indebted for this take on two of the soon-to-be cabinet shuffles to Donald, *Lincoln*, 550–51.
28. Nicolay and Hay, *Abraham Lincoln*, 9:386, 391.
29. Sumner, *Selected Letters*, 2:255.
30. Browne, *Every-Day Life of Abraham Lincoln*, 551.
31. Fehrenbacher and Fehrenbacher, *Recollected Words*, 499.
32. Browne, *Every-Day Life of Abraham Lincoln*, 551.
33. Rice, *Reminiscences of Abraham Lincoln*, 581.
34. Brooks, *Lincoln Observed*, 151.
35. Donald, *Lincoln*, 552.
36. Welles, *Diary*, 2:196.
37. Nicolay, *With Lincoln in the White House*, 166.

3. Advance and Retreat

1. Upson, *With Sherman to the Sea*, 139; Chambrun, *Impressions of Lincoln*, 7.
2. Sherman, *Memoirs*, 2:677.
3. Nicolay and Hay, *Abraham Lincoln*, 10:24.
4. Badeau, *Military History of Ulysses S. Grant*, 3:279.
5. Johnson and Buel, *Battles and Leaders*, 4:467.
6. Kelley, "Battle of Nashville," 34.
7. O.R, ser. 1, vol. 45, part 2, 180.
8. Angle and Miers, *Tragic Years*, 2:959.
9. Nicolay and Hay, *Abraham Lincoln*, 10:29.
10. Angle and Miers, *Tragic Years*, 2:964.
11. Strong, *Diary*, 530; Angle and Miers, *Tragic Years*, 2:965.
12. Watkins, *"Co. Aytch,"* 224.
13. Johnson and Buel, *Battles and Leaders*, 4:470.
14. Bates, *Lincoln in the Telegraph Office*, 318.
15. Lincoln, "To George H. Thomas," December 6, 1864, *Collected Works*, 8:169.
16. Fehrenbacher and Fehrenbacher, *Recollected Words*, 327.

17. Lyrics and Civil War rewrite of the song are from "The Yellow Rose of Texas (song)," *Wikipedia*, last modified January 6, 2014, http://en.wikipedia.org/wiki/The_Yellow_Rose_of_Texas_%28song%29.
18. Sherman, *Memoirs*, 2:700.
19. O.R., ser. 1, vol. 44, 783.
20. Lincoln, "To William T. Sherman," December 26, 1864, *Collected Works*, 8:181–82.
21. Ibid., 182n.
22. Sherman, *Memoirs*, 2:701–2.
23. Holzer and Symonds, *New York Times Complete Civil War*, 388.
24. Upson, *With Sherman to the Sea*, 145.
25. Strong, *Diary*, 531.
26. Chambrun, *Impressions of Lincoln*, 6.
27. *Annals of America*, 554.
28. Coffin, *Four Years of Fighting*, 393.
29. Chesnut, *Mary Chesnut's Civil War*, 694, 696; Nichols, *Story of the Great March*, 96.
30. This description of Fort Fisher is borrowed and recast from McPherson, *Battle Cry of Freedom*, 819.
31. Pearce, "Expeditions against Fort Fisher," 364, 366; Welles, *Diary*, 2:213.
32. Lamb, "Defence of Fort Fisher," 361–62.
33. Johnson and Buel, *Battles and Leaders*, 4:657.
34. Grant, *Personal Memoirs*, 2:574–75.
35. Lee, *Wartime Washington*, 460, 457.
36. Holzer and Symonds, *New York Times Complete Civil War*, 393.
37. *New York Herald*, November 17, 1864.
38. Welles, *Diary*, 2:221.
39. Harkness, "Expeditions against Fort Fisher and Wilmington,"163.
40. Lamb, "Defence of Fort Fisher," 371.
41. Johnson and Buel, *Battles and Leaders*, 4:647.
42. Pearce, "Expeditions against Fort Fisher," 380.
43. Johnson and Buel, *Battles and Leaders*, 4:648.
44. Ibid., 647.
45. Parker, "Navy in the Battles and Capture of Fort Fisher," 111.
46. Johnson and Buel, *Battles and Leaders*, 4:650, 650n.
47. Raymond, *Life and Public Services of Abraham Lincoln*, 642.
48. O'Flaherty, "The Blockade That Failed," 40.
49. Stephens, *Constitutional View of the Late War between the States*, 2:619, 620.

4. Confederacy on the Ropes

1. *Washington Star*, March 4, 1865.
2. Badeau, *Military History of Ulysses S. Grant*, 3:351.

3. *New York Herald*, November 17, 1864.
4. Adams, *Autobiography*, 165.
5. Kean, *Inside the Confederate Government*, 181.
6. Raymond, *Life and Public Services of Abraham Lincoln*, 647.
7. Upson, *With Sherman to the Sea*, 139.
8. Chesnut, *Mary Chesnut's Civil War*, 669, 674, 683.
9. Sherman, *Memoirs*, 2:702, 705, 718.
10. These plans are outlined in ibid., 749–53.
11. Lincoln, "To Ulysses S. Grant," January 19, 1865, *Collected Works*, 8:223, 223–24n.

5. Deathblow to Slavery

1. Fehrenbacher and Fehrenbacher, *Recollected Words*, 51.
2. Ibid., 280.
3. *Congressional Globe*, 38th Cong, 1st sess. (April 8, 1864), 1484.
4. Vorenberg, *Final Freedom*, 107.
5. *Congressional Globe*, 38th Cong., 1st sess., appendix, 113.
6. Arnold, *Life of Abraham Lincoln*, 356.
7. Raymond, *Life and Public Services of Abraham Lincoln*, 752.
8. The Republican platform is in *Proceedings of the First Three Republican National Conventions*, 225–26.
9. Lincoln, "Annual Message to Congress," December 6, 1864, *Collected Works*, 8:149.
10. Lee, *Wartime Washington*, 460.
11. Brooks, *Washington in Lincoln's Time*, 187.
12. Julian, *Political Recollections*, 251.
13. U.S. Constitution, Amendments, Article XIII.
14. Lincoln, "Response to a Serenade," February 1, 1865, *Collected Works*, 8:254–55; Fehrenbacher and Fehrenbacher, *Recollected Words*, 384.
15. Holzer and Symonds, *New York Times Complete Civil War*, 396.
16. Belz, *Emancipation and Equal Rights*, 113.
17. Lee, *Wartime Washington*, 453.
18. Schurz, *Speeches, Correspondence and Political Papers*, 1:5; Brooks, *Mr. Lincoln's Washington*, 411.
19. Whittier, "Laus Deo," 874.

6. Negotiating Peace

1. Donald, *Lincoln*, 555.
2. Smith, *Francis Preston Blair Family*, 2:303.
3. Blair's letter to Davis is in Lincoln, "Pass for Francis P. Blair, Sr.," December 28, 1864, *Collected Works*, 8:188–89n.
4. Townsend, *Campaigns of a Non-combatant*, 330.

5. Blair's visit is described in Kirkland, *Peacemakers*, 198, 199, 201, 245–46
6. Ibid., 222–23.
7. Lincoln, "To Francis P. Blair, Sr.," January 18, 1865, *Collected Works*, 8:220–21.
8. Lincoln's various actions and instructions leading to the negotiations are in Lincoln, "To the House of Representatives," February 10, 1865, *Collected Works*, 8:274–85.
9. Chesnut, *Mary Chesnut's Civil War*, 706–7.
10. Grant, *Personal Memoirs*, 2:591.
11. Nicolay, *Lincoln's Secretary*, 222.
12. Fehrenbacher and Fehrenbacher, *Recollected Words*, 420.
13. Lincoln, "To the Senate," February 10, 1865, *Collected Works*, 8:286–87n.
14. Holzer and Symonds, *New York Times Complete Civil War*, 399; Kirkland, *Peacemakers*, 257.
15. Kean, *Inside the Confederate Government*, 198.

7. With Malice toward None

1. Brown, *Raymond of the Times*, 255.
2. Raymond, *Life and Public Services of Abraham Lincoln*, 668, 669.
3. Lincoln, "Reply to the Notification Committee," March 1, 1865, *Collected Works*, 8:326.
4. Beckett, *War Correspondents*, 170.
5. Brooks, *Lincoln Observed*, 165.
6. Brooks, "Lincoln's Reelection," 870; *Mr. Lincoln's Washington*, 419.
7. Lincoln, "To Andrew Johnson," January 14, 1865, *Collected Works*, 8:217n.
8. Ibid., 235.
9. Sandburg, *Abraham Lincoln*, 6:101–2.
10. *New York Herald*, March 5, 1865.
11. Brooks, *Mr. Lincoln's Washington*, 424.
12. Fehrenbacher and Fehrenbacher, *Recollected Words*, 320.
13. Brooks, *Washington in Lincoln's Time*, 215.
14. *New York Herald*, March 6, 1865.
15. Brooks, *Washington in Lincoln's Time*, 195.
16. Browne, *Every-Day Life of Abraham Lincoln*, 557.
17. McBride, "Lincoln's Body Guard," 29.
18. Shakespeare, *Merchant of Venice*, act 4, sc. 1, lines 182–96.
19. The text of Lincoln's second inaugural is in *Collected Works*, 8:332–33.
20. Salmon P. Chase to Mary Todd Lincoln, March 4, 1865, Abraham Lincoln Papers.
21. Strong, *Diary*, 561.
22. Ford, *Cycle of Adams Letters*, 2:257–58.

23. Wilson, "Recollections of Lincoln," 528.
24. Mitgang, *Lincoln as They Saw Him*, 447.
25. Douglass, *Life and Times*, 801, 804.
26. Mitgang, *Lincoln as They Saw Him*, 440–41.
27. Lincoln, "To Thurlow Weed," March 15, 1865, *Collected Works*, 8:356.
28. *Washington Star*, March 4, 1865.
29. Sumner, *Selected Letters*, 2:284.
30. Brooks, *Lincoln Observed*, 169.

8. At the Seat of War

1. Johnson and Buel, *Battles and Leaders*, 4:684.
2. Ibid., 675.
3. This description of marching conditions is stitched from Nourse, "The Burning of Columbia," 440–41; Strong, *Diary*, 556; Force, "Marching across Carolina," 3, 8; and Johnson and Buel, *Battles and Leaders*, 4:687, 688–89.
4. Upson, *With Sherman to the Sea*, 150.
5. Sherman, *Memoirs*, 2:760.
6. Jones, *Heroines of Dixie*, 360, 367–68.
7. Sherman, *Memoirs*, 2:767.
8. Cozzens and Girardi, *New Annals of the Civil War*, 552.
9. Jones, *Rebel War Clerk's Diary*, 501.
10. Strong, *Diary*, 555.
11. Chesnut, *Mary Chesnut's Civil War*, 715, 717, 731, 737.
12. Cox, *March to the Sea*, 168n.
13. Sherman, *Memoirs*, 2:788, 789.
14. Hitchcock, *Marching with Sherman*, 265–66.
15. Swinton, *Campaigns of the Army of the Potomac*, 566.
16. Nevins, *War for the Union*, 4:263–64.
17. Nichols, *Story of the Great March*, 162, 35.
18. Swinton, *Campaigns of the Army of the Potomac*, 568.
19. Rice, *Reminiscences of Abraham Lincoln*, 177.
20. *Washington Star*, March 17, 1865.
21. Swinton, *Campaigns of the Army of the Potomac*, 570.
22. Lincoln, "Speech to One Hundred Fortieth Indiana Regiment," March 17, 1865, *Collected Works*, 8:360–61.
23. Lincoln, "To Ulysses S. Grant," March 3, 1865, *Collected Works*, 8:330–31.
24. Angle and Miers, *Living Lincoln*, 641–42.
25. Browning, *Diary*, 2:8.
26. Lincoln, "To Ulysses S. Grant," March 20, 1865, *Collected Works*, 8:367n, 367, 372n.
27. Merritt, "Appomattox Campaign," 109.
28. Catton, *Army of the Potomac*, 321.

29. Cadwallader, *Three Years with Grant*, 281–82.
30. Badeau, *Military History of Ulysses S. Grant*, 3:148.
31. Grant, *Personal Memoirs*, 592.
32. Badeau, *Military History of Ulysses S. Grant*, 3:451.
33. Bruce, "Capture and Occupation of Richmond," 122–23.
34. Walker, "Gordon's Assault on Fort Stedman," 21.
35. Brooks, *Mr. Lincoln's Washington*, 427–28.
36. Fehrenbacher and Fehrenbacher, *Recollected Words*, 22.

9. "This Means Victory"

1. Johnson and Buel, *Battles and Leaders*, 4:709.
2. Ibid.
3. Lyman, *Meade's Headquarters*, 327.
4. Stern, *End to Valor*, 119.
5. Johnson and Buel, *Battles and Leaders*, 4:711, 711n.
6. Stern, *End to Valor*, 147.
7. Lincoln, "To Mary Todd Lincoln," April 2, 1865, *Collected Works*, 8:382n.
8. Cadwallader, *Three Years with Grant*, 307.
9. Johnson and Buel, *Battles and Leaders*, 4:719.
10. Lincoln, "To Ulysses S. Grant" and "To Godfrey Weitzel," March 29, 1865, *Collected Works*, 8:376–77.
11. Lincoln, "To Edwin M. Stanton," March 30, 1865, and "To Mary Todd Lincoln," April 2, 1865, *Collected Works*, 8:377, 378n, 381.
12. The account of Mary's jealous outbursts is in Badeau, *Grant in Peace*, 356–65. Also see Turner and Turner, *Mary Todd Lincoln*, 206–8.
13. Lincoln, "To Edwin M. Stanton," April 2, 1865, *Collected Works*, 8:382–83.
14. Lincoln, "To Ulysses S. Grant," April 2, 1865, *Collected Works*, 8:383.
15. Grant, *Personal Memoirs*, 2:612.

10. Sitting in Davis's Seat

1. Harrison, *Recollections Grave and Gay*, 216.
2. Cozzens and Girardi, *New Annals of the Civil War*, 563.
3. *Washington Evening Whig*, April 5, 1865, reprinted in the *Washington Star*, April 8, 1865.
4. Coffin, *Four Years of Fighting*, 503.
5. Harrison, *Recollections Grave and Gay*, 208; the information about the rail lines in Richmond is from Lankford, *Richmond Burning*, 85.
6. Strong, *Diary*, 575–76, 577.
7. *Annals of America*, 9:557, 558.
8. *Washington Evening Whig*, April 6, 1865, reprinted in the *Washington Star*, April 11, 1865; Bruce, "Capture and Occupation of Richmond," 135.

9. Cozzens and Girardi, *New Annals of the Civil War*, 560, 572.
10. Johnson and Buel, *Battles and Leaders*, 4:725–26.
11. Prescott, "Capture of Richmond," 70, 68; *Washington Evening Whig*, April 5, 1865, reprinted in the *Washington Star*, April 8, 1865.
12. Nevins, *War for the Union*, 4:288.
13. Bruce, "Capture and Occupation of Richmond," 134.
14. Cozzens and Girardi, *New Annals of the Civil War*, 515, 516.
15. Adams, "Capture of Richmond," 251.
16. Porter, *Incidents and Anecdotes of the Civil War*, 294.
17. Harrison, *Recollections Grave and Gay*, 210, 212, 218.
18. Porter, *Incidents and Anecdotes of the Civil War*, 294.
19. The exchange between Lincoln and Stanton is in O.R., ser. 1, vol. 46, part 3, 509.
20. The descriptions of Washington celebrating the fall of Richmond and Mary Lincoln's reaction are drawn from Lee, *Wartime Washington*, 489; Brooks, *Mr. Lincoln's Washington*, 433, 434; French, *Witness to the Young Republic*, 469; Chambrun, *Impressions of Lincoln*, 66, 67; and Turner and Turner, *Mary Todd Lincoln*, 212.
21. *Chicago Journal*, April 3, 1865, reprinted in the *Washington Daily National Republican*, April 11, 1865.
22. Porter, *Incidents and Anecdotes of the Civil War*, 294–95.
23. This account of the voyage up the river to the landing is distilled from Nicolay and Hay, *Abraham Lincoln*, 10:216–19.
24. Porter, *Incidents and Anecdotes of the Civil War*, 295, 297.
25. Coffin, *Four Years of Fighting*, 510–11.
26. Randall and Current, *Lincoln the President*, 347.
27. Graves's account is in Angle and Miers, *Tragic Years*, 2:1021–22.
28. Lincoln's meetings with Campbell are recounted by Weitzel in Cozzens and Girardi, *New Annals of the Civil War*, 519.
29. Holzer, *Lincoln Anthology*, 760.

11. The Road to Appomattox

1. These messages to Weitzel and Grant are in Lincoln, "To Godfrey Weizel," April 6, 1865, and "To Ulysses S. Grant," April 6, 1865, *Collected Works*, 8:388, 389.
2. Chamberlain, *Passing of the Armies*, 208, 209, 225, 223.
3. Ibid., 219.
4. Lincoln, "To Edwin M. Stanton," April 7, 1865, and "To Ulysses S. Grant," April 7, 1865, *Collected Works*, 8:389, 392.
5. Wise, *End of an Era*, 437.
6. Nicolay and Hay, *Abraham Lincoln*, 10:191.
7. Harrison, *Pickett's Men*, 155.

8. Long, *Memoirs of Robert E. Lee*, 421.
9. The Grant-Lee exchanges leading to the surrender, excepting Venable's role, are stitched from personal accounts by Grant and Porter in Grant, *Personal Memoirs*, 2:623–27; Angle and Miers, *Tragic Years*, 2:1029–33; Johnson and Buel, *Battles and Leaders*, 4:729–33; and Porter, *Campaigning with Grant*, 459–68.
10. Johnson and Buel, *Battles and Leaders*, 4:743n.
11. Porter, *Campaigning with Grant*, 473. Most of the detail describing the meeting in the McLean house between Grant and Lee is from Porter's account, 472–86.
12. Grant, *Personal Memoirs*, 2:629.
13. Ibid., 630.
14. Porter, *Incidents and Anecdotes of the Civil War*, 314.
15. Porter, *Campaigning with Grant*, 486.
16. Grant, *Personal Memoirs*, 2:633.
17. *New York Herald*, April 10, 1865.
18. Porter, *Campaigning with Grant*, 492.
19. Andrews, *War-Time Journal of a Georgia Girl*, 171.
20. Cozzens and Girardi, *New Annals of the Civil War*, 575, 588.
21. *Annals of the War*, 150–51.
22. Johnson and Buel, *Battles and Leaders*, 4:728.
23. Fehrenbacher and Fehrenbacher, *Recollected Words*, 114, 131, 398.

12. War's End

1. Lincoln, "To Ulysses S. Grant," April 6, 1865, *Collected Works*, 8:388n, 388.
2. Seward, *Reminiscences of a War-Time Statesman*, 253.
3. Lee, *Wartime Washington*, 491.
4. Brooks, *Washington in Lincoln's Time*, 223.
5. Ibid., 224.
6. An account of this morning celebration by the *Washington Daily National Intelligencer*, April 11, 1865, along with Lincoln's response, is in Lincoln, "Response to Serenade," April 10, 1865, *Collected Works*, 8:393–94n.
7. Ibid., 394.
8. Brooks, *Mr. Lincoln's Washington*, 439, 440; and *Lincoln Observed*, 183, 185, 187, 273–74n.
9. Lincoln, "Last Public Address," April 11, 1865, *Collected Works*, 8:400; Chambrun, "Personal Recollections of Mr. Lincoln," 33.
10. Brooks, *Lincoln Observed*, 185.
11. Welles, *Diary*, 2:242.
12. Chambrun, *Impressions of Lincoln*, 93.
13. Hay, *Lincoln and the Civil War*, 108.

14. Fehrenbacher and Fehrenbacher, *Recollected Words*, 57.
15. The full text of Lincoln's speech on reconstruction in response to the serenade is in Lincoln, "Last Public Address," April 11, 1865, *Collected Works*, 8:399–405.
16. Kellogg, "Recollections," 333.
17. Sumner, *Selected Letters*, 2:284.
18. Mitgang, *Lincoln as They Saw Him*, 457.
19. Ibid., 457, 458, 459.
20. Hanchett, *Lincoln Murder Conspiracies*, 37.
21. Lincoln, "To Godfrey Weitzel," April 12, 1865, *Collected Works*, 8:406–7.
22. Raymond, *Life and Public Services of Abraham Lincoln*, 690; Lincoln, "Memorandum Respecting Reduction of the Regular Army," c. April 13, 1865, *Collected Works*, 8:408–9, 409n.
23. Lincoln, "Response to a Serenade," November 10, 1864, *Collected Works*, 8:101.
24. Fehrenbacher and Fehrenbacher, *Recollected Words*, 7, 351.
25. Nicolay, *Personal Traits of Abraham Lincoln*, 32–33.
26. Hay, *At Lincoln's Side*, 109, 132.
27. Riddle, *Recollections of War Times*, 330.
28. Stoddard, *Inside the White House in War Times*, 3.
29. This rundown on Lincoln's last day is culled from Miers, *Lincoln Day by Day*, 3:329–30.
30. Hay, *At Lincoln's Side*, 139.

Epilogue: The Grand Farewell

1. Brooks, *Mr. Lincoln's Washington*, 472.
2. Guernsey and Alden, *Harper's Pictorial History of the Civil War*, 789.
3. Brooks, *Mr. Lincoln's Washington*, 471, 472, 473, 475.
4. Chamberlain, *Passing of the Armies*, 365, 368–69.
5. Gaylord, "Wisconsin Adjutant General's Office," 329–30.
6. Chamberlain, "Last Review of the Army of the Potomac," 315, 316.
7. Poore, *Sixty Years in the National Metropolis*, 2:187; Hay, *At Lincoln's Side*, 130; Brooks, *Washington in Lincoln's Time*, 271; Nicolay and Hay, *Abraham Lincoln*, 10:334.
8. Whitman, "Specimen Days," 778.

SOURCES CITED

Adams, Charles Francis. *Charles Francis Adams, 1835–1915: An Autobiography.* 1916. Reprint, Westport, CT: Greenwood Press, 1973.

Adams, Silas. "Capture of Richmond, Virginia, April 3, 1865." In *War Papers Read before the Commandery of the State of Maine, Military Order of the Loyal Legion of the United States.* Vol. 3. 1908. Reprint, Wilmington, NC: Broadfoot, 1992.

Alexander, Edward Porter. *Fighting for the Confederacy: The Personal Recollections of General Edward Porter Alexander.* Edited by Gary W. Gallagher. Chapel Hill: University of North Carolina Press, 1989.

Andrews, Eliza Frances. *The War-Time Journal of a Georgia Girl, 1864–1865.* 1908. Reprint, Lincoln: University of Nebraska Press, 1997.

Angle, Paul M., and Earl Schenck Miers, eds. *The Living Lincoln: The Man, His Mind, His Times, and the War He Fought, Reconstructed from His Own Writings.* New Brunswick, NJ: Rutgers University Press, 1955.

———. *Tragic Years, 1860–1865: A Documentary History of the American Civil War.* 2 vols. New York: Simon & Schuster, 1960.

The Annals of America. Vol. 9, *The Crisis of the Union, 1858–1865.* Chicago: Encyclopaedia Brittanica, 1976.

The Annals of the War Written by Leading Participants North and South. Originally published in the *Philadelphia Weekly Times.* 1878. Reprint, Dayton: Morningside, 1988.

Arnold, Isaac N. *The Life of Abraham Lincoln.* Chicago: Jansen, McClurg, 1885.

Badeau, Adam. *Grant in Peace: From Appomattox to Mount McGregor.* Hartford, CT: S. S. Scranton, 1887.

———. *Military History of Ulysses S. Grant, from April, 1861, to April, 1865.* 3 vols. New York: D. Appleton, 1881.

Bates, David Homer. *Lincoln in the Telegraph Office: Recollections of the United States Military Telegraph Corps during the Civil War.* New York: Century, 1907.

Bates, Edward. "Diary of Edward Bates, 1859–1866." Edited by Howard K. Beale. In *American Historical Association Annual Report for 1930.* Washington, DC: Government Printing Office, 1933.

Beckett, Ian F. W. *The War Correspondents: The American Civil War.* London: Grange Books, 1997.

Belknap, Charles E. "Recollections of a Bummer." In *War Papers: Being Papers Read before the Commandery of the District of Columbia, Military Order of the Loyal Legion of the United States.* Vol. 2. 1897–1903. Reprint, Wilmington, NC: Broadfoot, 1993.

Belz, Herman. *Emancipation and Equal Rights: Politics and Constitutionalism in the Civil War Era.* New York: W. W. Norton, 1978.

Brooks, Noah. *Lincoln Observed: Civil War Dispatches of Noah Brooks.* Edited by Michael Burlingame. Baltimore: Johns Hopkins University Press, 1998.

———. "Lincoln's Reelection." *Century Magazine* 49 (April 1895): 865–72.

———. *Mr. Lincoln's Washington: Selections from the Writings of Noah Brooks, Civil War Correspondent.* Edited by P. J. Staudenraus. South Brunswick, NJ: Thomas Yoseloff, 1967.

———. "Personal Recollections of Abraham Lincoln." *Harpers New Monthly Magazine* 31 (July 1865): 222–30.

———. *Washington in Lincoln's Time.* Edited by Herbert Mitgang. New York: Rinehart, 1958.

Brown, Francis. *Raymond of the Times.* New York: W. W. Norton, 1951.

Browne, Francis Fisher. *The Every-Day Life of Abraham Lincoln: A Narrative and Descriptive Biography with Pen-Pictures and Personal Recollections by Those Who Knew Him.* Chicago: Browne & Howell, 1913.

Browning, Orville H. *The Diary of Orville Hickman Browning.* Edited by Theodore Calvin Pease and James G. Randall. 2 vols. Springfield: Illinois State Historical Society Library, 1927, 1933.

Bruce, George A. "The Capture and Occupation of Richmond." In *Papers of the Military Historical Society of Massachusetts.* Vol. 14, *Civil War and Miscellaneous Papers.* 1918. Reprint, Wilmington, NC: Broadfoot, 1990.

Cadwallader, Sylvanus. *Three Years with Grant: As Recalled by War Correspondent Sylvanus Cadwallader.* Edited by Benjamin P. Thomas. New York: Alfred A. Knopf, 1955.

Catton, Bruce. *The Army of the Potomac: A Stillness at Appomattox.* Garden City, NY: Doubleday, 1953.

Chamberlain, Joshua Lawrence. "The Last Review of the Army of the Potomac." In *War Papers Read before the Commandery of the State of Maine, Military Order of the Loyal Legion of the United States.* Vol. 3. 1908. Reprint, Wilmington, NC: Broadfoot, 1992.

———. *The Passing of the Armies: An Account of the Final Campaign of the Army of the Potomac, Based upon Personal Reminiscences of the Fifth Army Corps.* Dayton: Press of Morningside Bookshop, 1989.

Chambrun, Charles Adolphe de. *Impressions of Lincoln and the Civil War: A Foreigner's Account.* New York: Random House, 1952.

———. "Personal Recollections of Mr. Lincoln." *Scribner's Magazine* 13 (January 1893): 26–38.

Chesnut, Mary Boykin. *Mary Chesnut's Civil War.* Edited by C. Vann Woodward. New Haven, CT: Yale University Press, 1981.

Cleland, John E. "The Second March to the Ohio." In *War Papers Read before the Indiana Commandery, Military Order of the Loyal Legion of the United States*. 1898. Reprint, Wilmington, NC: Broadfoot, 1992.

Coffin, Charles Carleton. *Four Years of Fighting: A Volume of Personal Observation with the Army and Navy from the First Battle of Bull Run to the Fall of Richmond*. 1866. Reprint, New York: Arno Press, 1970.

Connolly, James A. *Three Years in the Army of the Cumberland: The Letters and Diary of Major James A. Connolly*. Edited by Paul M. Angle. Bloomington: Indiana University Press, 1959.

Cox, Jacob D. *The March to the Sea: Franklin and Nashville*. 1882. Reprint, Wilmington, NC: Broadfoot, 1989.

Cozzens, Peter, and Robert I. Girardi, eds. *The New Annals of the Civil War*. Mechanicsburg, PA: Stackpole Books, 2004.

Davis, Jefferson. *The Papers of Jefferson Davis*. Edited by Lynda Lasswell Crist, Barbara J. Rozek, and Kenneth H. Williams. Vol. 11. Baton Rouge: Louisiana State University Press, 2003.

Donald, David Herbert. *Lincoln*. New York: Simon & Schuster, 1995.

Douglass, Frederick. *Life and Times of Frederick Douglass Written by Himself*. In *Frederick Douglass: Autobiographies*. New York: Library of America, 1994.

Fehrenbacher, Don E., and Virginia Fehrenbacher, eds. *Recollected Words of Abraham Lincoln*. Stanford, CA: Stanford University Press, 1996.

Force, Manning F. "Marching across Carolina." In *Sketches of War History, 1861–1865: Papers Read before the Ohio Commandery of the Military Order of the Loyal Legion of the United States*. Vol. 1. 1888. Reprint, Wilmington, NC: Broadfoot, 1991.

Ford, Worthington Chauncey, ed. *A Cycle of Adams Letters, 1861–1865*. 2 vols. Boston: Houghton Mifflin, 1920.

French, Benjamin Brown. *Witness to the Young Republic: A Yankee's Journal, 1828–1860*. Edited by Donald B. Cole and John J. McDonough. Hanover, NH: University Press of New England, 1989.

Gaylord, Augustus. "In and Out of the Wisconsin Adjutant General's Office, 1862–1866." In *War Papers: Being Papers Read before the Commandery of the State of Wisconsin, Military Order of the Loyal Legion of the United States*. Vol. 2. 1896. Reprint, Wilmington, NC: Broadfoot, 1993.

Goodwin, Doris Kearns. *Team of Rivals: The Political Genius of Abraham Lincoln*. New York: Simon & Schuster, 2005.

Grant, Ulysses S. *The Papers of Ulysses S. Grant*. Edited by John Y. Simon. 20 vols. Carbondale: Southern Illinois University Press, 1967–1995.

———. *Personal Memoirs of U. S. Grant*. 2 vols. 1894. Reprint, New York: AMS Press, 1972.

Guernsey, Alfred H., and Henry M. Alden. *Harper's Pictorial History of the Civil War*. 1866. Reprint, New York: Fairfax Press, n.d.

Hanchett, William. *The Lincoln Murder Conspiracies.* Urbana: University of Illinois Press, 1983.

Harkness, Edson J. "The Expeditions against Fort Fisher and Wilmington." In *Military Essays and Recollections: Papers Read before the Commandery of the State of Illinois, Military Order of the Loyal Legion of the United States.* Vol. 2. 1894. Reprint, Wilmington, NC: Broadfoot, 1992.

Harrison, Mrs. Burton. *Recollections Grave and Gay.* New York: Charles Scribner's Sons, 1911.

Harrison, Walter. *Pickett's Men: A Fragment of War History.* 1870. Reprint, Gaithersburg, MD: Butternut Press, 1984.

Hay, John. *At Lincoln's Side: John Hay's Civil War Correspondence and Selected Writings.* Edited by Michael Burlingame. Carbondale: Southern Illinois University Press, 2000.

———. *Inside Lincoln's White House: The Complete Civil War Diary of John Hay.* Edited by Michael Burlingame and R. Turner Ettlinger. Carbondale: Southern Illinois University Press, 1997.

———. *Lincoln and the Civil War in the Diaries and Letters of John Hay.* Edited by Tyler Dennett. New York: Dodd, Mead, 1939.

Hitchcock, Henry. *Marching with Sherman: Passages from the Letters and Campaign Diaries of Henry Hitchcock.* Edited by M. A. DeWolfe Howe. 1927. Reprint, New Haven, CT: Yale University Press, 1995.

Holzer, Harold, ed. *The Lincoln Anthology: Great Writers on His Life and Legacy from 1860 to Now.* New York: Library of America, 2009.

Holzer, Harold, and Craig L. Symonds, eds. *The New York Times Complete Civil War, 1861–1865.* New York: Black Dog & Leventhal, 2010.

Hood, John Bell. *Advance and Retreat: Personal Experiences in the United States & Confederate States Armies.* Edited by Richard N. Current. Bloomington: Indiana University Press, 1959.

Hutchins, Morris C. "The Battle of Franklin, Tennessee." In *Sketches of War History, 1861–1865: Papers Prepared for the Commandery of the State of Ohio, Military Order of the Loyal Legion of the United States, 1896–1903.* Edited by W. H. Chamberlin, A. M. Van Dyke, and George A. Thayer. Vol. 5. 1903. Reprint, Wilmington, NC: Broadfoot, 1992.

Jenkins, James Howard. "Origin of the Famous War Song of John Brown." In *War Papers: Being Papers Read before the Commandery of the State of Wisconsin, Military Order of the Loyal Legion of the United States.* Vol. 4. 1914. Reprint, Wilmington, NC: Broadfoot, 1993.

Johnson, Robert Underwood, and Clarence Clough Buel, eds. *Battles and Leaders of the Civil War: Being for the Most Part Contributions by Union and Confederate Officers Based upon "The Century War Series."* 4 vols. Secaucus, NJ: Castle, n.d.

Johnson, Rossiter. *Campfire and Battlefield: An Illustrated History of the Campaigns and Conflicts of the Great Civil War.* 1894. Reprint, Slovenia: Trident Press International, 1999.

Jones, John B. *A Rebel War Clerk's Diary.* Edited by Earl Schenck Miers. New York: Sagamore Press, 1958.

Jones, Katharine M., ed. *Heroines of Dixie: Confederate Women Tell Their Story of the War.* 1955. Reprint, New York: Konecky & Konecky, n.d.

Julian, George W. *Political Recollections, 1840–1872.* Chicago: Jansen & McClury, 1884.

Kean, Robert Garlick Hill. *Inside the Confederate Government: The Diary of Robert Garlick Hill Kean.* Edited by Edward Younger. New York: Oxford University Press, 1957.

Kelley, Leverett M. "Battle of Nashville." In *War Papers: Being Papers Read before the Commandery of the District of Columbia, Military Order of the Loyal Legion of the United States.* Vol. 4. 1908. Reprint, Wilmington, NC: Broadfoot, 1993.

Kellogg, William Pitt. "The Recollections of William Pitt Kellogg." Edited by Paul M. Angle. *Abraham Lincoln Quarterly* 3 (September 1945): 319–39.

Kerr, Charles D. "From Atlanta to Raleigh." In *Glimpses of the Nation's Struggle: A Series of Papers Read before the Minnesota Commandery of the Military Order of the Loyal Legion of the United States.* Vol. 1. 1887. Reprint, Wilmington, NC: Broadfoot, 1992.

Kirkland, Edward Chase. *The Peacemakers of 1864.* 1927. Reprint, New York: AMS Press, 1969.

Lamb, William. "Defence of Fort Fisher, North Carolina." In *Papers of the Military Historical Society of Massachusetts.* Vol. 9, *Operations on the Atlantic Coast 1861–1865, Virginia 1862, 1864.* 1912. Reprint, Wilmington, NC: Broadfoot, 1989.

Lankford, Nelson. *Richmond Burning: The Last Days of the Confederate Capital.* New York: Viking, 2002.

Lee, Elizabeth Blair. *Wartime Washington: The Civil War Letters of Elizabeth Blair Lee.* Edited by Virginia Jeans Laas. Urbana: University of Illinois Press, 1991.

Lincoln, Abraham. *The Collected Works of Abraham Lincoln.* Edited by Roy P. Basler. 9 vols. New Brunswick, NJ: Rutgers University Press, 1953–1955.

———. Papers. Library of Congress, Washington, DC.

Long, A. L. *Memoirs of Robert E. Lee: His Military and Personal History.* 1886. Reprint, Secaucus, NJ: Blue & Grey Press, 1983.

Lyman, Theodore. *Meade's Headquarters, 1863–1865: Letters of Colonel Theodore Lyman.* Edited by George R. Agassiz. 1922. Reprint, Freeport, NY: Books for Libraries Press, 1970.

McBride, Robert W. "Lincoln's Body Guard: With Some Personal Recollections of Abraham Lincoln." *Indiana Historical Society Publications* 5 (1911): 1–39.

McPherson, James M. *Battle Cry of Freedom: The Civil War Era.* New York: Oxford University Press, 1988.

McWhirter, Christian. *Battle Hymns: The Power and Popularity of Music in the Civil War.* Chapel Hill: University of North Carolina Press, 2012.

Merritt, Wesley. "The Appomattox Campaign." In *War Papers and Personal Reminiscences, 1861–1865: Read before the Commandery of the State of Missouri, Military Order of the Loyal Legion of the United States.* Vol. 1. 1892. Reprint, Wilmington, NC: Broadfoot, 1992.

Miers, Earl Schenck, ed. *Lincoln Day by Day: A Chronology, 1809–1865.* 3 vols. Washington, DC: Lincoln Sesquicentennial Commission, 1960.

Milchrist, Thomas E. "Reflections of a Subaltern on the Hood-Thomas Campaign in Tennessee." In *Military Essays and Recollections: Papers Read before the Commandery of the State of Illinois, Military Order of the Loyal Legion of the United States.* Vol. 4. 1907. Reprint, Wilmington, NC: Broadfoot, 1992.

Mitgang, Herbert, ed. *Abraham Lincoln: A Press Portrait.* Chicago: Quadrangle Books, 1971.

———. *Lincoln as They Saw Him.* New York: Rinehart, 1956.

Nevins, Allan. *The War for the Union.* Vol. 4, *The Organized War to Victory, 1864–1865.* New York: Charles Scribner's Sons, 1971.

Nicolay, Helen. *Lincoln's Secretary: A Biography of John G. Nicolay.* New York: Longmans, Green, 1949.

———. *Personal Traits of Abraham Lincoln.* New York: Century, 1912.

Nicolay, John G. *With Lincoln in the White House: Letters, Memoranda, and Other Writings of John G. Nicolay, 1860–1865.* Edited by Michael Burlingame. Carbondale: Southern Illinois University Press, 2000.

Nicolay, John G., and John Hay. *Abraham Lincoln: A History.* 10 vols. New York: Century, 1909.

Nichols, George Ward. *The Story of the Great March, from the Diary of a Staff Officer.* New York: Harper & Brothers, 1865.

Nourse, Henry S. "The Burning of Columbia." In *Papers of the Military Historical Society of Massachusetts.* Vol. 9. 1912. Reprint, Wilmington, NC: Broadfoot, 1989.

O'Flaherty, Daniel. "The Blockade That Failed." *American Heritage* 6 (August 1955): 38–41, 104–5.

Parker, James. "The Navy in the Battles and Capture of Fort Fisher." In *Personal Recollections of the War of the Rebellion: Addresses Delivered before the Commandery of the State of New York, Military Order of the Loyal Legion of the United States.* Edited by A. Noel Blakeman. Vol. 2. 1897. Reprint, Wilmington, NC: Broadfoot, 1992.

Pearce, Charles E. "The Expeditions against Fort Fisher." In *War Papers and Personal Reminiscences, 1861–1865: Read before the Commandery of the State of Missouri, Military Order of the Loyal Legion of the United States.* Vol. 1. 1892. Reprint, Wilmington, NC: Broadfoot, 1992.

Poore, Ben Perley. *Perley's Reminiscences of Sixty Years in the National Metropolis.* 2 vols. Philadelphia: Hubbard Brothers, 1886.

Porter, David Dixon. *Incidents and Anecdotes of the Civil War.* New York: D. Appleton, 1885.

Porter, Horace. *Campaigning with Grant.* 1897. Reprint, New York: Konecky & Konecky, 1992.

Prescott, Royal B. "The Capture of Richmond." In *Civil War Papers Read before the Commandery of the State of Massachusetts, Military Order of the Loyal Legion of the United States.* Vol. 1. 1900. Reprint, Wilmington, NC: Broadfoot, 1993.

Proceedings of the First Three Republican National Conventions of 1856, 1860 and 1864. Minneapolis: Charles W. Johnson, 1893.

Randall, James G., and Richard N. Current. *Lincoln the President: Last Full Measure.* New York: Dodd, Mead, 1955.

Raymond, Henry J. *The Life and Public Services of Abraham Lincoln.* New York: Derby and Miller, 1865.

Rhodes, James Ford. *History of the United States from the Compromise of 1850 to the McKinley-Bryan Campaign of 1896.* 8 vols. 1892–1919. Reprint, Port Washington, NY: Kennikat Press, 1967.

Rice, Allen Thorndike, ed. *Reminiscences of Abraham Lincoln by Distinguished Men of His Time.* 1888. Reprint, New York: Haskell House, 1971.

Riddle, Albert Gallatin. *Recollections of War Times: Reminiscences of Men and Events in Washington, 1860–1865.* New York: G. P. Putnam's Sons, 1895.

Sandburg, Carl. *Abraham Lincoln: The War Years.* Vol. 4. Sangamon Edition. New York: Charles Scribner's Sons, 1943.

Schofield, John M. *Forty-Six Years in the Army.* 1897. Reprint, Norman: University of Oklahoma Press, 1998.

Schurz, Carl. *Speeches, Correspondence and Political Papers of Carl Schurz.* Edited by Frederic Bancroft. 6 vols. 1913. Reprint, New York: Negro Universities Press, 1969.

Seward, Frederick W. *Reminiscences of a War-Time Statesman and Diplomat, 1830–1915.* New York: G. P. Putnam's Sons, 1916.

Sexton, James Andrew. "The Observations and Experiences of a Captain of Infantry at the Battle of Franklin, November 30, 1864." In *Military Essays and Recollections: Papers Read before the Commandery of the State of Illinois, Military Order of the Loyal Legion of the United States.* Vol. 4. 1907. Reprint, Wilmington, NC: Broadfoot, 1992.

Shakespeare, William. *The Merchant of Venice*. New Haven, CT: Yale University Press, 1923.

Sherman, William T. *Memoirs of General W. T. Sherman*. 2 vols. New York: Library of America, 1990.

Smith, William Ernest. *The Francis Preston Blair Family in Politics*. 2 vols. New York: Macmillan, 1933.

Speed, Thomas. "The Battle of Franklin." In *Sketches of War History, 1861–1865: Papers Prepared for the Ohio Commandery, Military Order of the Loyal Legion of the United States*. Edited by Robert Hunter. Vol. 3. 1890. Reprint, Wilmington, NC: Broadfoot, 1991.

Stephens, Alexander H. *Constitutional View of the Late War between the States: Its Causes, Character, Conduct and Results*. 2 vols. Philadelphia: National Publishing Company, 1870.

Stern, Philip Van Doren. *An End to Valor: The Last Days of the Civil War*. Boston: Houghton Mifflin, 1958.

Stoddard, William O. *Inside the White House in War Times: Memoirs and Reports of Lincoln's Secretary*. Edited by Michael Burlingame. Lincoln: University of Nebraska Press, 2000.

Strong, George Templeton. *The Diary of George Templeton Strong: The Civil War, 1860–1865*. Edited by Allan Nevins and Milton Halsey Thomas. New York: Macmillan, 1952.

Sumner, Charles. *The Selected Letters of Charles Sumner*. Edited by Beverly Wilson Palmer. 2 vols. Boston: Northeastern University Press, 1990.

Swinton, William. *Campaigns of the Army of the Potomac: A Critical History of Operations in Virginia, Maryland and Pennsylvania from the Commencement to the Close of the War, 1861–65*. 1866. Reprint, Secaucus, NJ: Blue & Grey Press, 1988.

Townsend, George Alfred. *Campaigns of a Non-combatant and his Romaunt Abroad during the War*. New York: Blelock, 1866.

Turner, Justin G., and Linda Levitt Turner. *Mary Todd Lincoln: Her Life and Letters*. New York: Alfred A. Knopf, 1972.

Upson, Theodore F. *With Sherman to the Sea: The Civil War Letters, Diaries & Reminiscences of Theodore F. Upson*. Edited by Oscar Osburn Winther. 1958. Reprint, New York: Kraus Reprint Company, 1969.

U.S. War Department. *The War of the Rebellion: A Compilation of the Official Records of the Union and Confederate Armies*. 70 vols. in 128 parts. 1880–1901. Reprint, Harrisburg, PA: Historical Times, 1985.

Vorenberg, Michael. *Final Freedom: The Civil War, the Abolition of Slavery, and the Thirteenth Amendment*. Cambridge, England: Cambridge University Press, 2001.

Wainwright, Charles S. *A Diary of Battle: The Personal Journals of Colonel Charles S. Wainwright, 1861–1865*. Edited by Allan Nevins. New York: Harcourt, Brace & World, 1962.

Walker, James A. "Gordon's Assault on Fort Stedman." In *Southern Historical Society Papers*. Vol. 31. 1903. Reprint, Millwood, NY: Kraus Reprint Company, 1979.

Watkins, Sam R. *"Co. Aytch": A Side Show of the Big Show*. Introduction by Bell Irwin Wiley. 1882. Reprint, Wilmington, NC: Broadfoot, 1990.

Welles, Gideon. *Diary of Gideon Welles*. 3 vols. Boston: Houghton Mifflin, 1911.

Whitman, Walt. "Specimen Days." In *Walt Whitman: Complete Poetry and Collected Prose*. New York: Library of America, 1982.

Whittier, John Greenleaf. "Laus Deo." In *American Antislavery Writings: Colonial Beginnings to Emancipation*. Edited by James G. Basker. New York: Library of America, 2012.

Wilson, James Grant. "Recollections of Lincoln." *Putnam's Magazine* 5 (February, March 1909): 515–29, 670–75.

Wise, John Sergeant. *The End of an Era*. Edited by Curtis Carroll Davis. New York: Thomas Yoseloff, 1965.

INDEX

An italicized *f* after a page number indicates a figure.

John C. Waugh, a reporter at the *Christian Science Monitor* for many years, is the coeditor of *How Historians Work* and the author of a dozen other books on the Civil War era, including *The Class of 1846*, *Reelecting Lincoln*, *One Man Great Enough*, *Surviving the Confederacy*, and *Lincoln and McClellan*.

This series of concise books fills a need for short studies of the life, times, and legacy of President Abraham Lincoln. Each book gives readers the opportunity to quickly achieve basic knowledge of a Lincoln-related topic. These books bring fresh perspectives to well-known topics, investigate previously overlooked subjects, and explore in greater depth topics that have not yet received book-length treatment. For a complete list of current and forthcoming titles, see www.conciselincolnlibrary.com.

Other Books in the Concise Lincoln Library

Abraham Lincoln and Horace Greeley
Gregory A. Borchard

Lincoln and the Civil War
Michael Burlingame

Lincoln's Sense of Humor
Richard Carwardine

Lincoln and the Constitution
Brian R. Dirck

Lincoln in Indiana
Brian R. Dirck

Lincoln the Inventor
Jason Emerson

Lincoln and Native Americans
Michael S. Green

Lincoln and the Election of 1860
Michael S. Green

Lincoln and Congress
William C. Harris

Lincoln and the Union Governors
William C. Harris

Lincoln and the Abolitionists
Stanley Harrold

Lincoln's Campaign Biographies
Thomas A. Horrocks

Lincoln in the Illinois Legislature
Ron J. Keller

Lincoln and the Military
John F. Marszalek

Lincoln and Emancipation
Edna Greene Medford

Lincoln and the American Founding
Lucas E. Morel

Lincoln and Reconstruction
John C. Rodrigue

Lincoln and the Thirteenth Amendment
Christian G. Samito

Lincoln and Medicine
Glenna R. Schroeder-Lein

Lincoln and the Immigrant
Jason H. Silverman

Lincoln and the U.S. Colored Troops
John David Smith

Lincoln's Assassination
Edward Steers, Jr.

Lincoln and Citizenship
Mark E. Steiner

Lincoln and Race
Richard Striner

Lincoln and Religion
Ferenc Morton Szasz with Margaret Connell Szasz

Lincoln and the Natural Environment
James Tackach

Lincoln as Hero
Frank J. Williams

Abraham and Mary Lincoln
Kenneth J. Winkle